O

# Managing the Linux kernel with AgentX

Oliver Wellnitz

# Managing the Linux kernel with AgentX

## Design and Implementation

VDM Verlag Dr. Müller

Bibliographic information by the German National Library: The German National Library lists this publication at the German National Bibliography; detailed bibliographic information is available on the Internet at http://dnb.d-nb.de.

Copyright © 2007 VDM Verlag Dr. Müller e. K. and licensors
All rights reserved. Saarbrücken 2007
Contact: info@vdm-verlag.de
Cover image: www.purestockx.com
Publisher: VDM Verlag Dr. Müller e. K., Dudweiler Landstr. 125 a, 66123 Saarbrücken, Germany
Produced by: Lightning Source Inc., La Vergne, Tennessee/USA
          Lightning Source UK Ltd., Milton Keynes, UK

Bibliografische Information der Deutschen Nationalbibliothek: Die Deutsche Nationalbibliothek verzeichnet diese Publikation in der Deutschen Nationalbibliografie; detaillierte bibliografische Daten sind im Internet über http://dnb.d-nb.de abrufbar.

Copyright © 2007 VDM Verlag Dr. Müller e. K. und Lizenzgeber
Alle Rechte vorbehalten. Saarbrücken 2007
Kontakt: info@vdm-verlag.de
Coverbild: www.purestockx.com
Verlag: VDM Verlag Dr. Müller e. K., Dudweiler Landstr. 125 a, 66123 Saarbrücken, Deutschland
Herstellung: Lightning Source Inc., La Vergne, Tennessee/USA
          Lightning Source UK Ltd., Milton Keynes, UK

ISBN: 978-3-8364-1285-8

## Abstract

Network management is essential for the operation and supervision of medium to large computer networks. The *Simple Network Management Protocol (SNMP)* is the standard protocol for network management in the Internet. Ordinary SNMP agents are mostly monolithic and implement all information, the *Managed Objects*, in a single program. The concept of subagents makes it possible to delegate the implementation of *Managed Objects* to several subagents. All subagents are managed by a master agent.

This thesis examines to what extent the IETF standard subagent protocol AgentX is suitable for the management of UNIX kernel components. For this purpose, subagents have been implemented within the kernel subsystem they manage. They use the AgentX protocol for communication with the master agent in userspace. The implemented software contains a generic sublayer which can carry out AgentX protocol operations and variable manipulation. On top of this layer two kernel subsystems have been enhanced with management extensions.

## Kurzfassung

Netzwerkmanagement ist für den Betrieb und die Überwachung mittlerer bis großer Computernetze unverzichtbar. Das *Simple Network Management Protocol (SNMP)* ist das Standardprotokoll für Netzwerkmanagement im Internet. Herkömmliche SNMP Agenten sind dabei meistens monolithisch und implementieren alle Informationen, die sogenannten *Managed Objects*, in einem einzelnen Programm. Das Konzept der Subagenten erlaubt es nun die Implementation von *Managed Objects* auf mehrere solche Subagenten zu verteilen, die alle von einem Master Agenten verwaltet werden.

Diese Arbeit untersucht inwieweit das IETF Standard-Subagentenprotokoll AgentX für das Management von Komponenten eines UNIX Kernels geeignet ist. Hierzu werden die Subagenten direkt in der zu verwaltenden Komponente im Kernel implementiert und kommunizieren mit einem Master Agenten im Userspace. Die im Laufe der Arbeit erstellte Implementation beinhaltet eine generische Zwischenschicht, die AgentX Protokolloperationen und Variablenmanipulationen durchführen kann. Darauf aufsetzend werden zwei Kernelkomponenten exemplarisch mit Managementerweiterungen ausgestattet.

# Contents

# List of Figures

# List of Tables

# 1 Introduction

*Even goldfish can be taught to play the piano,*
*if you use enough voltage.*
— Jeffrey D. Case

## 1.1 Motivation

Network management is essential for the operation and supervision of medium to
large computer networks and the Simple Network Management Protocol (SNMP[1])
is the standard network management protocol of the Internet. Current implementations of this protocol are mostly monolithic and rarely extensible. SNMP agents cover
a broad spectrum of management information from application-specific and protocol-
dependent data (e.g. HTTP-MIB) to low-level and system-dependent data (e.g. Interfaces MIB).

Linux SNMP agents which implement system-dependent management information
usually are userspace programs. They gather information from the operating system's
core, the kernel, through different means such as special system calls, device driver
input/output control functions (ioctls) and the /proc filesystem. These kernel interfaces are difficult to handle because, for example, one has to parse a file in the /proc
filesystem which has a structure that may change in time. They also can be incomplete
in respect to the MIB which is to be implemented. Furthermore, SNMP notifications
cannot be created efficiently because there is no kernel notification mechanism in the
methods mentioned above. So whenever an SNMP agent wants to handle notifications,
it has to use polling to gather information and detect changes itself. This strategy has
two flaws: If the polling interval is set too small, polling data from the kernel wastes
CPU time. On the other hand, setting the polling interval too high, the data in question
may change two or more times during that time and a change cannot be detected accurately. Another problem with currently available SNMP agents is that they must know
specific details about every component they implement. So why not let the component's manufacturer implement his parts, because he knows his device best? An agent
developer may even choose to implement only a basic subset and let the component's
manufacturer decide if he wants to override it with his own improved subagent for his
component or not.

AgentX kernel subagents may overcome these problems, because a kernel implementation of AgentX gives programmers the opportunity to implement network management code within the kernel subsystem at low cost. Hence, they do not rely on interfaces but have access to every kernel data structure and the ability to add new ones if necessary. They can also be synchronously and accurately triggered upon changes because they do not sit in a process in userspace which has to poll for changes. In the kernel subagents can be implemented inside the subsystem and detect changes directly, or they can get values just after they were polled from a device or make the process send out a notification when it changes data through a system call.

## 1.2 Scope

The goal of this thesis is to analyze and elaborate the AgentX subagent architecture for Linux kernel subsystems. Although the implementation developed here requires an AgentX master agent to operate, the master agent is not implemented during this project. Instead we use the SNMP daemon of the NET-SNMP project[2] as the master agent and keep the focus on the kernel subagent components. The software implemented during this project is to be understood as a proof of concept and should therefore not be used on production systems. The subagents, that were created here, are designed as network management extensions for their respective kernel subsystems and may represent only a partial MIB.

## 1.3 Structure

After this introduction, the next chapter discusses the AgentX protocol which defines a standardized framework for extensible SNMP agents. It takes a close look at every AgentX protocol data unit (PDU) and shows examples for the most common transactions. Other subagent protocols are briefly described and a short comparison closes the second chapter. The AgentX implementation for the Linux kernel is described in the third chapter. It shows the design and the implementation of the generic AgentX layer and the network management extensions, the MIB modules. Examples show and explain the interaction of all management functions. This chapter also contains a short introduction on how to compile and use the Linux Kernel AgentX implementation. Two implemented MIBs are described in the fourth chapter. It shows code samples and explains the different implementation strategies which are the basis for these network management extensions. Finally, the fifth and last chapter summarizes the ideas and considerations of this thesis and gives an outlook.

## 1.4 Acknowledgement

Many people helped and supported me during the last six months and in the following I would like to point out a few. First of all, I would like to express my gratitude to Frank Strauß and Prof. Dr. Stefan Fischer, who gave me the opportunity to write about this interesting topic and who never got tired answering all of my questions.

I would like to extend my thanks to the following people, who have been helpful during my work:

- Jürgen Schönwälder for his suggestions to some implementation topics and for his inspiring comments that he gave me on every occasion.

- Aiko Pras, who made me think about writing in English.

- Jeff Dike, the developer of User-Mode Linux which made kernel development a lot easier to test and to debug.

Frank Strauß, Lars Horeis and Holger R. Gode proofread this paper and gave me invaluable feedback. As always, all remaining errors and deficiencies are my own.

# 2 SNMP Subagent Protocols

*The man who can't spell a word more than one way lacks creativity.*
— W.C. Fields

In the past 15 years the number of network-capable devices increased dramatically. Today's companies and organizations do not have a single but a whole bunch of inter-connected local area networks (LANs) each consisting of heterogeneous components such as hosts, routers, printers, etc. Such a large number of systems cannot be managed manually by network administrators, so there is a very real need for a management technology spoken by all kinds of systems. In the Internet this network management technology is the Simple Network Management Protocol (SNMP) framework. There are also other network management protocols, e.g. CMIP[3], but they are well beyond the scope of this document.

SNMP[4] contains three primary elements: an SNMP manager, SNMP agents and an information database, called management information base (MIB). The manager is the console through which the network administrator performs network management functions. Agents are the entities with an interface to the actual device or service being managed. The Managed Objects are variables that represent components of hardware, configuration parameters, performance statistics, or other things that directly relate to the current operation of the device in question. They are arranged in a management information base. SNMP allows managers and agents to communicate for the purpose of accessing these objects. A more in depth look at SNMP can be found in [5] and [6].

## 2.1 AgentX

### 2.1.1 Overview

Developed as a protocol to dynamically extend SNMP agents, Agent eXtensibility (AgentX) was published in January 2000 on IETF's standard track as RFC2741[7].

The AgentX framework splits the role of an agent into two separate entities:

- a master agent, which is a traditional SNMP agent but with little or no direct access to management information, and

5

- a set of subagents, which have access to a mostly disjunct set of management information and no knowledge about SNMP.

Master agent and subagent communicate through the AgentX protocol. The master agent thereby acts as multiplexer and SNMP ↔ AgentX protocol translator for the subagents. AgentX is transparent to SNMP managers and SNMP independent, which means that AgentX subagents can be combined with SNMPv1, SNMPv2c and SN-MPv3 master agents. Figure 2.1 shows the interaction between the components.

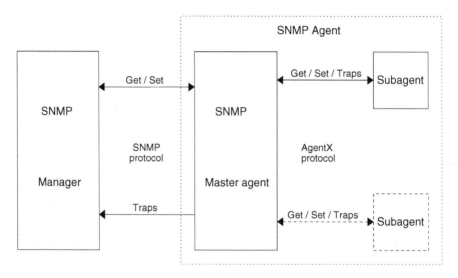

Figure 2.1: Manager, agent and subagent interaction

The AgentX protocol was designed to be simple in respect of authorization, privacy and encoding. It completely leaves the first two points to the master agent, which has to ensure that only allowed mangers can access or change management information. Encoding looks different from the subagent's point of view because there is no need for SNMP's BER/ASN.1 coding. While trying to keep AgentX simple, it also offers full support for data retrieval (SNMP Get, GetNext and GetBulk) and data modification operations (SNMP Set) as well as notifications (SNMP traps). With a multiphase-commit SNMP Set operations remain atomic even if the Set request has to be spread among several subagents.

The advantages of such a protocol are obvious. This way the whole management system can be more flexible and each subagent can be closer to the managed information, which means "do only one thing, but do it well".

## 2.1.2 The Protocol

AgentX transport mappings are specified for Unix domain sockets and the Transmission Control Protocol (TCP), Port 705. Any other IPC-like transport mechanisms are likewise conceivable. A connection can be split up into several sessions, which in turn can convey several transactions. Figure 2.2 shows the interaction of connections, sessions and transactions.

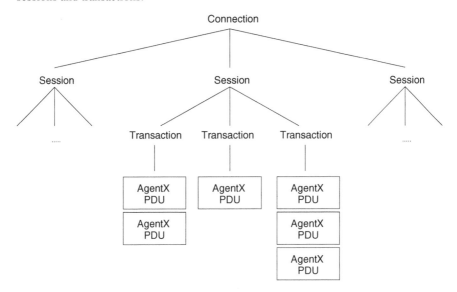

Figure 2.2: AgentX connection hierarchy

Different AgentX PDUs can contain different payloads which are not shown in this figure. Especially worth mentioning payloads are variable bindings (VarBinds) and SearchRanges.

AgentX consists of 18 different packet types or protocol data units (PDUs), which can be differentiated into three types:

- 9 administrative PDUs,

- 8 data PDUs and

- 1 generic response PDU.

A generic 20 octet packet header (see Figure 2.3) is common to all packets. This header contains the protocol version, the PDU type, a flag field, the payload length and

IDs for the session, transaction and packet. For performance reasons all AgentX PDUs are 32-bit aligned.

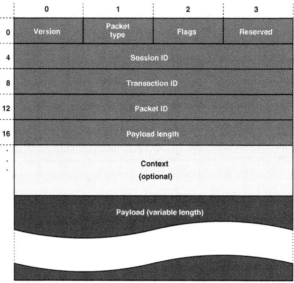

Figure 2.3: An AgentX packet

The individual PDUs are to be regarded now in detail:

**AgentX Open PDU**                                    **(administrative, subagent only)**

This PDU is used by the subagent to open a session to the master agent. The creation of a session is normally the first step after a connection was established. A connection may contain more than one session.

**AgentX Close PDU**                                    **(administrative, both)**

An AgentX Close PDU terminates a session. It can be used by either the subagent or the master agent.

**AgentX Register PDU**                                    **(administrative, subagent only)**

With an AgentX Register PDU the subagent claims responsibility for a certain region of the MIB tree. This region can be a subtree or just a single object. Registering a row in a MIB table is also supported. A priority field shows the precedence if several subagents register the same or overlapping regions. A subagent may send more than one Register PDUs per session in order to register different MIB regions.

## AgentX Unregister PDU                    (administrative, subagent only)

The subagent revokes responsibility for a previously registered MIB region by sending an Unregister PDU.

## AgentX Get PDU                                    (data, master agent only)

One or more data objects can be retrieved with a Get PDU. Every data object must be specified with its exact object identifier.

## AgentX GetNext PDU                                (data, master agent only)

An AgentX GetNext PDU can be used to get one or more data objects. In addition to a Get request, it is not necessary to specify an exact object identifier for each data object. Instead, a SearchRange can be defined, which consists of two OIDs. The first OID defines the start point and the second OID defines the end point of the range. The subagent selects the closest lexicographical successor to the starting point. The search for the successor must not be extended beyond an optional given search end.

## AgentX GetBulk PDU                                (data, master agent only)

An AgentX GetBulk PDU is basically split into two areas, *Non-repeaters* and *Repeaters*, each consisting of a group of SearchRanges. Non-repeaters are processed exactly as for the GetNext PDU. Repeaters do not have just one but several successor data objects. The exact number of data objects for each Repeater is configurable within the GetBulk PDU. AgentX GetBulk PDUs can be more efficient than GetNext PDUs when several successive OIDs are requested.

## AgentX TestSet PDU                                (data, master agent only)

The master agent can prepare the change of one or more data objects by sending a TestSet PDU. When several data objects are to be written and they do not fit in one PDU, they can be split up into several TestSet PDUs. Upon receiving such a PDU the subagent checks the validity of types and values and reports the result back to the master agent. The first TestSet PDU defines the start of a new Set transaction.

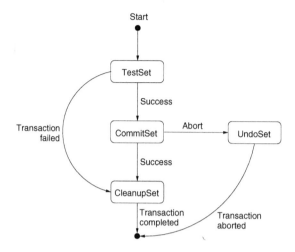

Figure 2.4: AgentX Set transaction states

## AgentX CommitSet PDU                                      (data, master agent only)

A CommitSet PDU triggers the actual writing of variables previously prepared by a TestSet PDU. It is sent by the master agent, if all previous TestSets were successful. A Set transaction may be completed with either an UndoSet or CleanupSet PDU.

## AgentX UndoSet PDU                                         (data, master agent only)

The master agent can abort a Set transaction by sending an UndoSet PDU. Thereupon the subagent undoes the previous actions triggered by a CommitSet PDU.

## AgentX CleanupSet PDU                                      (data, master agent only)

A CleanupSet PDU successfully terminates a Set transaction with a subagent. The master agent sends this PDU when the transaction is successfully completed or to signal a failed transaction when one or more TestSets returned an error. This PDU does not result in a Response PDU.

## AgentX Notify PDU                                          (data, subagent only)

This PDU is sent by the subagent to forward an asynchronous notification through the master agent. A Notify PDU then causes the transmission of an SNMP Trap or SNMP

Inform PDU in the master agent. AgentX notifications must contain `snmpTrapOID.0` as one of the first variables.

## AgentX Ping PDU                                (administrative, subagent only)

To monitor the master agent's ability to receive and send AgentX PDUs, the subagent can send a Ping PDU. It resembles the ICMP echo request[8] but is answered with a standard AgentX response packet instead of an echo reply.

## AgentX IndexAllocate PDU                       (administrative, subagent only)

A subagent can use an IndexAllocate PDU to allocate one or more MIB table rows. It may request reservation of a specific table row, a row that is not currently allocated or a row that has never been allocated. Index allocation does not imply any MIB tree registration.

## AgentX IndexDeallocate PDU                     (administrative, subagent only)

A subagent may release a previously allocated index by sending an IndexDeallocate PDU.

## AgentX AddAgentCaps PDU                        (administrative, subagent only)

This PDU is used by the subagent to inform the master agent of agent capabilities for the session. An agent capability is an SNMP feature and describes the level of support which an agent claims in regard to a MIB. Agent capabilities are discussed in detail in [9].

## AgentX RemoveAgentCaps PDU                     (administrative, subagent only)

An agent capability previously advertised by the subagent can be revoked through the use of a RemoveAgentCaps PDU.

## AgentX Response PDU                            (generic response, both)

Almost every administrative and data request PDU is answered with an AgentX Response PDU. It contains an error status and an error index field, which indicate if and where an error has occurred. If the original request contained any MIB variables, these data objects are appended to the Response PDU.

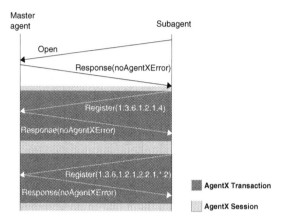

Figure 2.5: AgentX connection example

## 2.1.3 Examples

This section shows examples of some typical AgentX protocol transactions. First a connection to the master agent is opened and some MIB branches are registered. Then data is transmitted through Get, Set and Notification messages.

### Establishing a Connection

After opening a Unix domain or TCP socket and creating a session, the AgentX subagent must register with the master agent. Figure 2.5 shows a subagent which opens a session and registers two MIB branches.

At first the subagent initiates a session by sending an AgentX Open PDU to the master agent. The master agent then assigns a new session ID and sends a Response PDU in reply. If no error occurred during this opening phase, a new session has been established which can be used for data transactions. In order to receive Get/Set requests from the master agent, the subagent has to register the MIB variables it wants to provide first. In this example the subagent registers the whole IP MIB (1.3.6.1.2.1.4) which is then acknowledged by the master agent with a Response PDU. The next Register PDU requests the second table row of the interface table (ifTable) from the IF-MIB because the subagent wants to be responsible for the management of the interface that is identified by ifIndex 2. After further acknowledgement by the master agent the session is operational and the two MIB branches are registered.

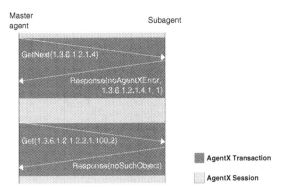

Figure 2.6: AgentX data retrieval example

## Retrieving Data

When the master agent receives an SNMP Get request from a manager, it has to search for the responsible subagent, translate this request into AgentX and forward the translated message. This procedure is also the same for SNMP GetNext and GetBulk messages. The example in Figure 2.6 shows a GetNext and a Get request, which ask for a single variable each. The GetNext request is successful and the subagent answers with the variable's OID and its value. The Get request asks for the second interface, column 100 in IF-MIB's ifTable, which does not exist. So the subagent returns an error.

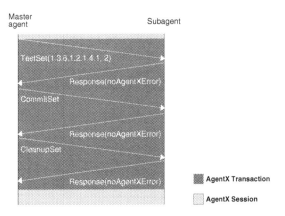

Figure 2.7: AgentX Set operation example

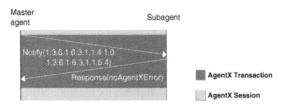

Figure 2.8: AgentX notification example

### Modifying Data

AgentX Set operations (see figure 2.7) are executed in three phases: A test phase and a two-phase commit. This partition is necessary because in SNMP Set operations are atomic and AgentX preserves this property, even when the OIDs specified in a Set request are registered by different subagents. First there is one or more AgentX TestSet PDU which are checked for validity and accessibility by the subagent to ensure that a subsequent CommitSet operation can be carried out successfully. This CommitSet message then causes the actual modification of the data. Finally a Set transaction must be completed with either a CleanupSet PDU which approves the changes, or an Undo-Set PDU which rolls the whole transaction back. Only the master agent can do Set operations and each session can only handle a single Set transaction at a time.

### Sending Notifications

Notifications, or traps as they are called in SNMP, are only sent by the subagent. The master agent simply translates and forwards the message to its SNMP trap sink. Figure 2.8 shows an example of such a notification. A response which does not indicate an error means that the Notify PDU was processed successfully by the master agent. It does mean that neither the SNMP trap was sent successfully nor that the trap sink received the message.

## 2.2 Other Concepts

AgentX is not the first protocol that deals with the problem of extending SNMP agents. In the following we take a look at some other, mostly older protocols and their differences compared to AgentX.

## 2.2.1 SNMP MUX

In 1991 the SNMP multiplexing protocol[10], SMUX for short, was introduced. It simply extends the SNMP protocol with new administrative PDUs to open and close connections and to register MIB branches with subagents, so called SMUX peers. The architecture defines two ways of operation. First, the request-response approach, which is said to be agent-driven, because the SNMP agent initiates all transactions. In this model, the SNMP agent forwards all SNMP packets for a registered MIB region to the SMUX peer. The peer performs the operation and returns a response, which in turn the SNMP agent sends back to the requestor. Second, the cache-ahead model, where the SMUX peer periodically sends updates of his management information to the SNMP agent. With any method a password may restrict subagent access to the master agent during the opening phase. SMUX can be transported over any connection-orientated service but was defined for TCP (port 199) only.

## 2.2.2 Distributed Program Interface

The Distributed Program Interface (DPI) was published in 1991[11] and revised in 1994 as version 2.0[12]. Like AgentX, DPI does not use SNMP and ASN.1 but has its own encoding and packet protocol with open, close, register and several Get and Set PDUs. However, it lacks index allocation and SNMP agent capability support. During connection establishment, a DPI subagent can authenticate against the master agent if required. DPI works with any transport service either connection-orientated or connection-less. Thereby the subagent has to use SNMP GetRequest to ask the master agent for the dynamic DPI port number.

## 2.2.3 EMANATE

EMANATE is the abbreviation for Enhanced MANagement Agent Through Extensions and is a product[13] of SNMP Research Inc. Although the protocol details are available under NDA only, there is free information about what EMANATE is capable of. A subagent can register MIB branches or table rows (index allocation) but the protocol provides a method of priority on a per-subagent basis only. Data transfer between subagents is also possible as the subagent can send Get requests through the master agent. EMANATE works with Unix domain sockets, TCP or as a shared library.

## 2.2.4 Comparison

The following table (Table 2.1) compares all four subagent protocols which were discussed before.

| | SMUX | DPI | EMANATE | AgentX |
|---|---|---|---|---|
| Transportation service: | | | | |
| - connection-orientated | X | X | X | X |
| - connection-less | | X | | |
| Simplified encoding | | X | X | X |
| Multiple sessions | | | | X |
| Branch allocation | | X | X | X |
| Index allocation | | | X | X |
| GetBulk request | | X | X | X |
| Agent Capabilities | | | | X |

Table 2.1: Comparison between distributed network management protocols

This comparison shows the development of subagent protocols and the trend towards connection-orientated protocols and simple encoding. The SNMP multiplexing protocol offers little improvements for subagents in regard to SNMP. EMANATE is more advanced but it is a commercial product with an inappropriate license for the Linux kernel. The AgentX protocol was heavily influenced by the DPI 2.0 specification and it is the sole open and standardised subagent protocol.

# 3 Design and Implementation

*I still think we should just switch to a 100,000*
*second day and to hell with the sun.*
— Peter da Silva

This chapter introduces the reader to the implementations of the basic AgentX infrastructure and network management extensions for the Linux kernel. However, procedures and methods on how to program the Linux kernel are not discussed here. A good introduction on this topic can be found in [14] and [15]. After this overview, we take a closer look at the two basic Linux AgentX components. Finally the implementation is described based on some examples.

The implementation is divided into two parts:

- a generic AgentX sublayer (AgentX module), which is MIB-unaware but omniscient in regard to the AgentX protocol and its variable types and

- one or more management entities with access to management information and their structure (MIB module(s)).

The AgentX sublayer is a separate piece of software which is to protect the MIB module programmer from as many AgentX protocol details as possible. At the same time it offers helper functions which can be used to create, alter and transform special variable types used by AgentX protocol, e.g., modify or create object identifiers (OID). It must, however, place no restrictions on the interface so that a MIB module is able to do everything it could do if it would implement the AgentX protocol stack by itself. The short version for this is: Put everything possible into the AgentX sublayer but not more. Additionally its ease of use should encourage maintainer of kernel subsystems to implement network management functionality within their subsystem.

While the AgentX sublayer treats OIDs only as a sequence of numbers, MIB modules know the meaning of each OID. They also know how to get information from existing kernel data structures and how to put them into AgentX variables. Furthermore they use existing kernel-internal notification methods for kernel subsystems or create new ones to detect interesting status changes. With Set transactions they examine the values of the new variables for consistency and do range checking. It is common that

17

subagents implement one whole MIB at a time but as the AgentX protocol supports different levels of registration a MIB module can use this variety.

The Linux kernel can be extended in two different ways. First of all, new code can be statically linked with the kernel, so whenever you change any part, it has to be rebuilt and you have to reboot your machine. The other way is to extend the running kernel with functionality and to load and unload subsystems on demand (kernel modules). This implementation supports both kinds, thus the AgentX subsystem and the MIB modules can either be linked with the kernel or built as kernel modules. It should be noted that all MIB modules depend on the AgentX module. That means that whenever the AgentX subsystem is built as a kernel module, every MIB module has to be compiled likewise.

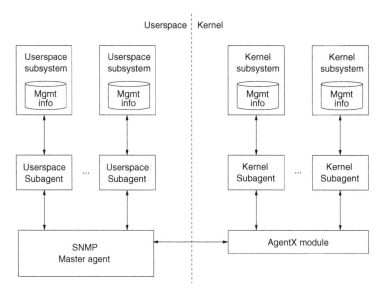

Figure 3.1: SNMP/AgentX framework overview

Figure 3.1 gives an overview of the SNMP AgentX framework with kernel extensions. We focus on the kernel elements on the right side, the userspace subagents are added for the sake of completeness and are not to be regarded any further.

## 3.1 The AgentX Module

The AgentX module is a mediator between the master agent and the MIB modules. It has the protocol knowledge to talk to the master agent in userspace and the knowledge of all available MIB modules which have access to management information. In doing so, it is tried to extensively relieve the individual MIB modules from protocol tasks. Figure 3.2 divides the AgentX module into its basic parts.

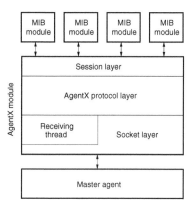

Figure 3.2: AgentX module overview

The socket layer forwards all AgentX packets from the upper protocol layer to the master agent. Its interface is very small and can easily be exchanged or modified to support other AgentX transport methods. Currently Unix domain sockets and, for debugging reasons, TCP are implemented. While sending data can be done immediately, receiving data is more difficult because one cannot use blocking operations inside the kernel. So, as a result, receiving data is done in a kernel thread.

The AgentX protocol layer is able to parse received AgentX packets and build new ones, which are then sent through the socket layer to the master agent. It also enforces the AgentX protocol specification, so that MIB modules are not bothered with invalid packets and only valid packets are sent to the master agent. It was tried to solve as much as possible generically in the protocol layer, thereby the subagent can attend to its actual task, i.e., supplying management information. When the protocol layer receives a request from the master agent, it divides this request into smaller pieces, which are simpler to process by the subagent. E.g., if a GetNext request contains more than one SearchRange, the AgentX module creates an empty Response PDU, takes the first SearchRange and dispatches it to the corresponding MIB callback function. Then the answer from the callback function is appended to the Response PDU. This procedure is repeated until all SearchRanges were processed. Because of this, the callback function does not need to know anything about SearchRanges or Repeaters (see Get-Next/GetBulk PDU descriptions on page 9 for an explanation on SearchRanges and Repeaters). The AgentX module serializes all such requests.

The session layer decides which MIB module gets a request from the master agent and which session a response belongs to. For this purpose, every MIB module has to register with the session layer prior to communicating with the master agent. Additionally to the registration methods the AgentX protocol offers, the session layer implements a finer grained registration to delegate MIB subtrees to different functions of the MIB module.

## 3.1.1 The MIB Interface

As mentioned before, the interface between the AgentX and the MIB module has been designed to handle as much as possible generically in the AgentX sublayer. The interface consists of 22 functions which can be divided into four basic groups. A more accurate description of each interface function can be found in Appendix B.

1. **Administrative functions** (3)
   Administrative functions handle all preliminary tasks when a subagent and the master agent want to exchange data. Functions to open and close a session fall under this category as well as registering an OID range. A subagent can unregister an OID range if it closes the corresponding session to the master agent, so there is no explicit unregister function. Examples for this group are `ax_session_open()` and `ax_register()`.

2. **OID functions** (11)
   Object identifiers are introduced as an abstract data type and therefor several functions to create, modify and compare OIDs are needed. Converting functions, e.g., embedding a string in an OID, also belong to this category. Examples for this group are `ax_oid_cmp()` and `ax_oid_addstring()`.

3. **Time functions** (2)
   Time functions make the master agents' value of `sysUptime` available to subagents. The following section covers this topic in detail. The two time functions are `ax_time_now()` and `ax_time_jiffies()`.

4. **Low-level / direct access functions** (6)
   Low-level functions allow direct access to AgentX protocol functions. They can be used to create an AgentX PDU, add payload of different types, send a PDU and finally free it. These functions are needed for notification messages, because these messages are somewhat different compared to other AgentX PDUs. Notification PDUs create the sole subagent-initiated data transaction in the AgentX protocol. They also can contain an undetermined number of variable bindings of different types. Examples of this category are `ax_createpdu_notify()` and `ax_send_pdu()`.

## 3.1.2 Time Handling

There are different options to express time in terms of an SNMP/AgentX variable. One of them is the so called TimeStamp, that measures time in milliseconds relative to the time the master agent was started. This starting time is stored in `sysUptime.0`. TimeStamp is a textual convention and is explained in [16].

There are several occasions where one would need this value in a MIB implementation. One example is `ifTableLastChange` in the Interfaces MIB (`IF-MIB`). In Linux kernel AgentX we use the fact that every Response PDU sent by the master agent contains the current value of `sysUptime`. When a Response PDU arrives from the master agent, the value of `sysUptime` and the kernel time variable `jiffies` are stored together. If later on, a MIB module needs to know the current value of `sysUptime`, it can simply be calculated.

*HZ* is defined as the increase of the variable *jiffies* in one second.

$$\text{HZ} := \frac{\text{jiffies}}{s}$$

$$\text{TimeStamp} = \text{stored.TimeStamp} + \frac{\text{jiffies} - \text{stored.jiffies}}{\text{HZ}} \times 100$$

Because the protocol requires that an AgentX Open PDU is always answered with an Response PDU, we can be sure that this method works after the first session was opened. Normally Linux kernel AgentX and the master agent run on the same host, so we can calculate the value of `sysUptime` exactly. To prevent divergence between Linux kernel AgentX and the master agent on separate hosts when using a TCP connection, the AgentX module updates its calculation base every time it receives a Response PDU.

## 3.2 A MIB Module

A MIB module implements some network management functionality. It registers itself and its OID ranges with the AgentX module. It communicates with the master agent mainly by the use of a high-level API, which protects the MIB module from AgentX protocol details. It therefore allows kernel programmers inexperienced with AgentX to write their network management extensions easily.

Figure 3.3 shows the two different designs of MIB modules. First of all, one can closely integrate it with the existing code, using its functions and adding a few new ones. These new functions should be enclosed by `ifdefs` so that the system administrator can decide at compile-time whether he wants network management support for this subsystem or not. The second option is to develop the extension separately.

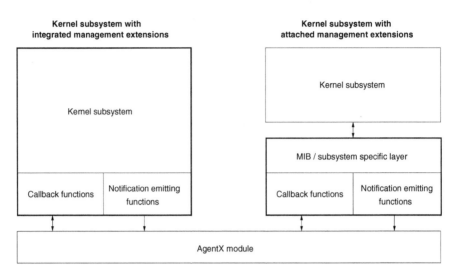

Figure 3.3: MIB module overview

The maintainer of the original code adds points where the network management part can hook into, hence the extension can be built as an additional kernel module and maintained separately.

The callback functions are registered with the AgentX module and are called from there for all Get and Set requests. The notification emitting functions are activated by other kernel functions when certain events happen, so they can send out a notification message. When management functionality is implemented within the kernel subsystem, notifications can usually be triggered in functions that really do the data change. When implemented as a standalone network management module, it depends on the kernel subsystem to offer notification hooks. As a result, embedding the MIB module in the kernel subsystem is preferable, because it does not depend on the subsystem in such a way. When the MIB module is not integrated within the kernel subsystem, it needs an additional layer to implement notifications and/or access information inside the subsystem.

## 3.2.1 MIB Callback Functions

MIB callback functions do not need to know AgentX protocol details. As seen before, they get fed with small requests by the AgentX module. This is how the signature of a MIB callback function looks like:

```
int cbfunction(ax_oid *oid, ax_method method,
```

```
                  char* context, ax_variable *res)
```

The callback function requires a single request OID and a method as arguments. Additionally, the SNMP *context* and a pointer to the VarBind structure *res* for the result are handed over. The callback function returns an error code (see page 46 for a list of error codes). The variable *oid* is the start OID of a SearchRange or the OID of a VarBind and always lies within the area that the callback function has registered. When the AgentX module receives an AgentX GetNext PDU and dispatches the first SearchRange, it compares the first OID of that SearchRange (start OID) to the callback function's registration point. If the start OID is a lexicographical predecessor compared to the registration point, it uses the registration point as value for the variable *oid* and sets the INCLUDE flag in the *method* variable. Hence, the callback function can safely assume that *oid* is always its registration point or a lexicographical successor. With that approach, finding a successor to an OID is simpler. When subOID regions for the callback functions overlap, the order in the `ax_cb_table` data structure decides. The first callback function that returns a valid answer wins.

MIB callback functions can be called in five different ways. A single Get method and four methods for Set transactions (TestSet, CommitSet, UndoSet and CleanupSet). Additionally the variable *method* can hold two flags which describe the interpretation of the OID variable *oid* (INCLUDE and EXACT). The flag INCLUDE means that the search range includes *oid* itself, if it is not set *oid* is excluded. The flag EXACT means that the request is for the exact *oid*, not a successor. Table 3.1 shows how SearchRanges from AgentX Get, GetNext and GetBulk requests are translated into callback function methods. AgentX GetBulk Repeaters are transformed into several non-repeating SearchRanges which are separately dispatched to the MIB callback functions. This is useful, because for GetBulk Repeaters the results can come from different callback functions.

| AgentX PDU | Callback function method |
|---|---|
| Get | GET & EXACT |
| GetNext | GET or GET & INCLUDE |
| GetBulk (Non-repeater) | GET or GET & INCLUDE |
| GetBulk (Repeater) | (GET or GET & INCLUDE)* |

Table 3.1: AgentX PDU type to method translation

## 3.3 Examples

This section shows and explains the functionality of the AgentX module and its interface with a set of examples. First of all, a MIB module opens a connection to the

23

master agent, which thereupon conducts a Get request and a Set transaction. Finally the MIB module sends out a notification. Code examples can be found in the manual pages in Appendix B.

## 3.3.1 Preparations

Before a MIB module can transfer any data, it has to open a session with the AgentX module using `ax_session_open()` (see page 49 for details). Thereby the description of the MIB module, a timeout value for the session and an optional callback function for status notifications are transferred. The AgentX module now calls the internal function `ax_session_create()` to add this new session to the list of all sessions and `ax_session_openpdu()` to actually send an AgentX Open PDU to the master agent. Sending an Open PDU may be delayed if there is no established connection to the master agent. All sessions are opened as soon as the AgentX module is in contact with the master agent.

The next thing the MIB module will do is to register its OID subtrees with `ax_register()`. Please note that we do not have an established session with the master agent yet. What we are doing here is hiding the real status from the MIB module, so it does neither know whether the session already has been established nor if there even is a master agent that it can talk to. It can just safely assume that the master agent is there and is listening, the AgentX sublayer will take care of the rest.

The function `ax_register()` takes the data structure `ax_register_table` as argument, that contains a pointer to the table `ax_register_cb`. Table 3.5 shows all registration data structures and pointers. The registration data structure `ax_register_table` contains among other things the point of registration in the OID tree (*root*) and OID bounds. The point of registration represents the common prefix of all OIDs of all MIB objects. When using OID bounds, a subagent can, e.g., register a table row with a single PDU. The variable *range* is set to zero when registering MIB trees. Other values indicates MIB range allocation. The registration structure also contains a pointer to a table of subOIDs and their callback functions. SubOIDs are a convenient way to distribute tasks to several callback functions without the need for one big dispatcher within each MIB module. Instead it is done generically in the AgentX module. The following example shows how the callback function OIDs are determined:

The MIB module sets the variable *root*, its point of registration, to the mib-2.interfaces tree (`1.3.6.1.2.1.2`). The callback table contains subOIDs `2.1.2` and `2.1.3` and pointers to their according callback functions (see Figure 3.5).

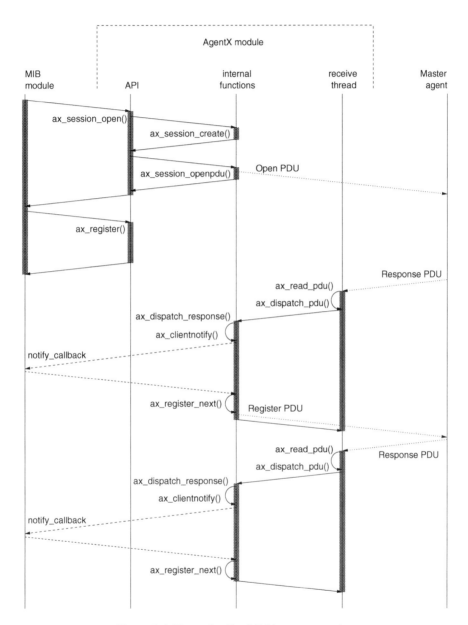

Figure 3.4: Example: Establishing a connection

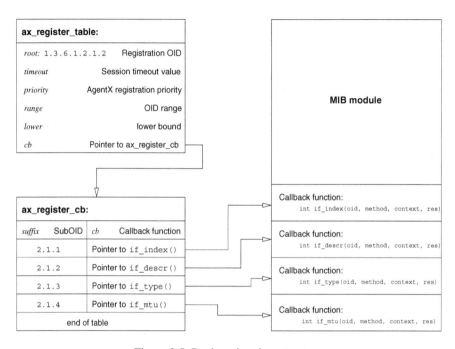

Figure 3.5: Registration data structure

| session registration | + | subOID | = | registered callback function |
|---|---|---|---|---|

$$\underbrace{1.3.6.1.2.1.2}_{\text{interfaces}} \quad + \quad 2.1.2 \quad = \quad \underbrace{1.3.6.1.2.1.2.2.1.2}_{\text{interfaces.ifTable.ifEntry.ifDescr}}$$

$$\underbrace{1.3.6.1.2.1.2}_{\text{interfaces}} \quad + \quad 2.1.3 \quad = \quad \underbrace{1.3.6.1.2.1.2.2.1.3}_{\text{interfaces.ifTable.ifEntry.ifType}}$$

So these functions are responsible for the interface descriptions and the interface types, respectively the table row `ifDescr` and `ifType`. When subOIDs register different levels in the OID tree, it is possible that the individual subOID ranges overlap. The AgentX module's dispatcher is described in detail in the next section.

The rest of the registration process is triggered by the master agent. When a response to the initial Open PDU arrives, the AgentX sublayer marks the corresponding session as open and starts registering the OID subtrees, previously registered by the MIB module. The internal function `ax_register_next()` takes care of this part. The registration is done step by step, so the master agent doesn't get flooded with Register PDUs when the link between it and the AgentX module becomes active.

It is necessary that the Response PDU is received asynchronously, because we cannot wait for an answer inside the kernel. If we would do so, it may never happen, because there is no multitasking there and the master agent would never have a chance to get a free CPU slot to send an answer.

Every status change on any session or registration can result in calling a notification callback function in the corresponding MIB module. The reasons for this include a successfully established session with the master agent or the reply from the master agent when the MIB module has sent a Register PDU. A complete list of notification reasons can be found in the manual pages for ax_session_open() on page 49. So if a module really wants to know all the details, the AgentX sublayer will tell. Please note that Figure 3.4 and all further example figures are simplifications and among other things, completely leave out the socket layer.

## 3.3.2 Processing Get/GetNext/GetBulk Requests

These requests are initiated by the master agent. Figure 3.6 shows an example of a GetNext request which is very similar to the processing of a Get or GetBulk request. After receiving, the AgentX packet is parsed, which is not shown in this figure, and the function ax_dispatch_getnext() looks for the corresponding session.

It then dispatches every SearchRange contained in the GetNext request to ax_dispatch_sr(). This SearchRange dispatcher now iterates over all callback functions for this session and assembles their registration OIDs as described in the preceding section. These OIDs are compared to the starting and ending OID in the given SearchRange. If they are within this range, the GetNext request is dispatched to the corresponding callback function. This procedure is repeated until a callback function returns a valid result or the end of the callback function table is reached. This is done for all SearchRanges in the request. A Get request is processed in the same way. But for every dispatched SearchRange, the INCLUDE flag is set . GetBulk requests contain non-repeating SearchRanges which are dispatched in the same way as GetNext requests. Repeaters are dispatched several times. On each iteration the starting OID is replaced with the OID of the previous result and the INCLUDE flag is cleared.

In this example, the first callback function does not meet the requirements of the SearchRange and therefore is not called. The second function does match the criteria but cannot serve an object within the SearchRange. For this reason, it returns 'No such object'. The following two functions again do not lie within the SearchRange and so the request is dispatched to the fifth callback function, which returns a valid OID and its value. This result is reported back to ax_dispatch_getnext() which sends it back to the master agent.

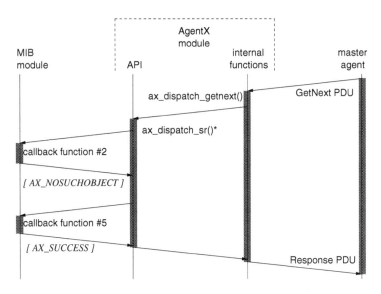

Figure 3.6: Example: Processing a GetNext request

### 3.3.3 Processing a Set Transaction

The AgentX protocol accomplishes a Set transaction in three phases (see Figure 2.4). This is done to preserve the atomic nature of an SNMP Set request. However for the AgentX module, Set transactions are very similar to Get requests, because the dispatching is done in the same way. In case of success, a Set transaction consists of three request PDUs: A TestSet PDU to prepare the write access, a CommitSet PDU to actually write the data and a CleanupSet PDU to finish the transaction.

One or more TestSet PDU initiate the Set transaction and every VarBind is dispatched to the MIB module's callback functions. They check the VarBinds for type correctness and value range as well as if the given OID allows write access at all. The AgentX module saves all VarBinds from the TestSet PDUs because they are needed later. When all TestSet PDUs were processed successfully, the master agent sends a CommitPDU to actually trigger the data change. Because a CommitPDU does not contain any additional data, the AgentX module has to refer to the previously saved VarBind list to dispatch the CommitSet PDU to all corresponding MIB callback functions. When the transaction is successfully finished, the master agent sends a CleanupSet PDU and again the AgentX module has to rely on its saved VarBind list to tell the MIB callback functions that the Set transaction is complete.

Because only one Set transaction is allowed at a time, the AgentX module can store the VarBind list of the transaction easily. As mentioned before, the dispatcher for Set

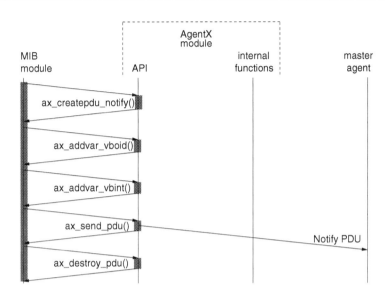

Figure 3.7: Example: Sending a notification

transactions is very similar to the dispatcher for Get requests. However, there is a small difference. In contrast to Get requests, Set transaction PDUs contain VarBinds and not SearchRanges. So when handling Set transaction PDUs, a single VarBind is dispatched to the MIB callback function.

## 3.3.4 Sending a Notification

Notifications are more complicated from the MIB module author's point of view. Because of the nature of Notify PDUs, the interface is more low-level than the others seen before (see Figure 3.7). At first the MIB module creates a Notify PDU with ax_createpdu_notify(). Then it may add an arbitrary number of VarBinds to this PDU with ax_addvar_vb*(). The MIB module may add as many variable bindings (VarBinds) as necessary within the limit of the maximum AgentX packet size. When finished, the packet is sent with ax_send_pdu() and its memory is released with ax_destroy_pdu().

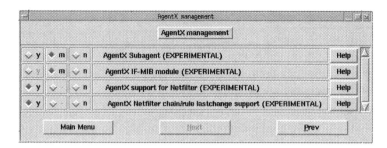

Figure 3.8: Kernel configuration

# 3.4 Using Linux Kernel AgentX

After patching the Linux kernel source tree with the AgentX patch, some configuration options are added under the topic '*AgentX management*' (see Figure 3.8).

- **AgentX Subagent**
  This option enables the AgentX subsystem. It can be build into the kernel or as a kernel module. If built as a kernel module, all other parts that use the AgentX module also have to be built as modules.

- **AgentX IF-MIB module**
  This option activates the implementation of the interfaces MIB (IF-MIB). It can be built independently from networking support because it is a standalone kernel network management module. The kernel must, of course, support networking. A detailed description of this option can be found on page 33.

- **AgentX support for Netfilter**
  This option adds support for the Linux Netfilter MIB. As a matter of course, Netfilter support must also be enabled to use this option. This implementation supports all tables and built-in chains as well as user-defined chains. It however lacks IPv6 support as well as extension matches and targets. A detailed description of this option can be found on page 35.

- **AgentX Netfilter chain/rule lastchange support**
  This option enables support for the LastChange time elements in the Linux Netfilter MIB. Because the original Netfilter subsystem does not support the recording of timestamps, the userspace tool '*iptables*' has to be rebuild against the new kernel headers if this option is used.

After a reboot the AgentX subsystem does not know when the master agent is ready to receive. So the AgentX module has to be told when to connect to the master agent.

However MIB subagents can connect to the AgentX module at any time. Open and Register PDUs are delayed until the AgentX module has established a connection to the master agent. The activation of the AgentX subsystem can be done with

```
# echo 1 >/proc/sys/kernel/agentx/running
```

The AgentX module now connects to the master agent and registers all subagents which have registered themselves with the AgentX module so far. If for any reason a connection to the master agent cannot be established, the AgentX module falls back to disconnected mode and you can try to connect later. If you compiled AgentX as a kernel module, you have to stop the receiving kernel thread and remove all other AgentX capable kernel modules prior to unloading the AgentX module itself. This can be done with the following command:

```
# echo 0 >/proc/sys/kernel/agentx/running
```

After this command is executed, the AgentX module can be unloaded safely. However, you can start it again at any time. When compiled directly into the kernel, the AgentX sublayer can be disconnected from the master agent but it cannot be unloaded.

# 4 Implemented MIB Modules

*The sun rises, the sun sets, the Sun crashes.*
*[...] It is the way of things.*
— Steve Conley

To complete the Linux AgentX framework, MIB modules had to be implemented. During this project two MIB modules were created: Implementations of the IETF standard interface MIB (IF-MIB[17]) and the proprietary Linux Netfilter MIB. The first one is a separate network management module which can be compiled as a kernel module only. So it can be loaded and unloaded at will. It does not change any kernel data structures and uses existing functions to access information in the kernel. Additional data is stored separately in the module itself. The IF-MIB was chosen, because it is a common MIB and already implemented in NET-SNMP's agent. Hence, we can compare the potential of these implementations and draw conclusions on the advantages and flaws of the AgentX framework. Additionally, we can use the IF-MIB implementation to test priority registering, because we use the NET-SNMP agent as master agent which also has an implementation of the IF-MIB. The Netfilter MIB implementation is experimental and Linux-specific. It extends existing kernel code with network management functions. Data structures were changed in order to allow the storage of additional information necessary to the MIB. We now take a closer look at both implementations.

## 4.1 Interfaces MIB

The interface MIB describes objects used for managing network interfaces. This implementation accesses existing kernel data structures directly or through functions provided by the Linux networking code, especially for the use in other parts of the kernel. It can notice changes of network interfaces through an already existing hook, which makes the module-only design feasible.

However, there are two variables which do not exist in the kernel: the time of change of an interface and the value of `ifLinkUpDownTrapEnable`. The latter is to specify whether to send an AgentX notification if an interface changes its status. Because a kernel module cannot extend existing data structures, the IF-MIB module introduces an interface shadow list where these values are stored. The elements of this list are created

33

```
int getmtu(int id) {
        int result = 0;
        struct net_device *dev;

        read_lock(&dev_base_lock);
        dev = __dev_get_by_index(id);
        if (dev)
                result = dev->mtu;
        read_unlock(&dev_base_lock);
        return result;
}
```

Figure 4.1: IF-MIB: MIB specific function

on demand so that the list only contains interfaces which have non-default values on any of these two variables. The defaults are zero for ifTableLastChange, which means that the last time of change was before the master agent was started, and one for ifLinkUpDownTrapEnable which means 'enabled'. In addition to read access, this module implements notifications for linkUp and linkDown and write access to ifLinkUpDownTrapEnable and ifAdminStatus.

Figure 4.1 shows an example of the MIB specific function getmtu(). It takes the interface ID as argument and uses an internal function of the networking subsystem to get the device pointer for the interface. It then returns the Maximum Transfer Unit (MTU) of the interface or zero, if the interface does not exist.

When the AgentX module receives a Get or Set request from the master agent, it dispatches this PDU to the corresponding callback function. Figure 4.2 shows an example of such a callback function. It covers the table row ifMtu, the Maximum Transfer Unit of all interfaces. The interfaces MIB describes this variables as read-only, so this function returns an error on all Set transactions. The function get_ifid() finds the correct interface ID for the requested OID or its successor in case of a GetNext request. The previously seen subsystem-specific function getmtu() is called to get the MTU of the interface. Finally the correct OID, type and value is reported back to the AgentX module.

| Area | Lines of code | Percent |
|---|---:|---:|
| MIB / Kernel subsystem specific | 406 | 44 % |
| Callback functions | 367 | 40 % |
| Notification functions | 51 | 5 % |
| Other | 101 | 11 % |
| Total | 925 | 100 % |

Table 4.1: Code distribution in MIB module IF-MIB

```
int if_mtu(ax_oid *oid,
        ax_method method,
        char* context,
        ax_variable *res)
{
        u_int32_t ifid;
        const ax_oid IFMTU =
                {10, {1, 3, 6, 1, 2, 1, 2, 2, 1, 4}};

        if (!(method & GET))
                return AX_NOTWRITABLE;

        ifid = get_ifid(oid, method, 4);
        if (!ifid)
                return AX_NOSUCHOBJECT;

        res->oid                = ax_oid_addint(IFMTU, ifid);
        res->type               = AX_VB_INT;
        res->value.integer      = getmtu(ifid);

        return AX_SUCCESS;
}
```

Figure 4.2: IF-MIB: Callback function for `ifMtu`

Table 4.1 shows the amount of line of code in each section of the MIB module. The kernel subsystem specific part implements access functions to the kernel interface table and the previously mentioned interface shadow list. Notifications for the IF-MIB are cheap and this group mainly consists of a single function which can send both implemented notifications (`linkUp` and `linkDown`). A callback function exists for each table row, which means there are many of them. The process of finding a lexicographical successor to an OID is also a difficult problem, so the callback functions make up half of the MIB module. The final ten percent are used by includes, comments and module initialisation.

## 4.2 Linux Netfilter MIB

The second implemented MIB is the TUBS IBR Linux Netfilter MIB. Netfilter is part of the Linux kernel networking code. It is the subsystem for packet filtering, mangling and network address translation (NAT). There is no standard MIB for Netfilter, so an experimental MIB (see Appendix C) was developed for this thesis.

The Linux Netfilter subsystem consists of one or more tables. There are currently three tables in the Linux kernel:

35

- **filter** (INPUT, FORWARD and OUTPUT chain)
  The packet filtering table.

- **nat** (PREROUTING, OUTPUT and POSTROUTING chain)
  The network address translation table.

- **mangle** (PREROUTING and OUTPUT chain)
  This table is used for specialized packet alteration.

Each table contains a number of built-in chains and may additionally have user-defined chains. The Netfilter subsystem currently has five hooks at five different points where an IP packet can traverse (INPUT, FORWARD, OUTPUT, PREROUTING and POST-ROUTING). So a table can have up to five different built-in chains. Every chain consists of a list of rules. Each rule consists of one or more conditions (matches) and an action (target). If a packet matches all conditions, the according target is applied. Each build-in chain has a default policy which decides the fate of an IP packet that does not match any rule. More information on the Linux Netfilter subsystem can be found in [18].

The Linux Netfilter subsystem is divided into several modules, which are responsible for different tasks. One module handles all table and chain management (`ip_-tables.c`), and so all according network management functionality can be implemented there. This module introduces data structures for Netfilter's tables and chains and some functions to do sanity checks but it, e.g., lacks methods to access a specific chain. This is done in userspace by Netfilter's configuration tool *iptables(1)*[19]. This is usually a good thing to do because it keeps the kernel code small, but makes the task of adding AgentX network management code more difficult. So existing userspace functions had to be rewritten and put into the kernel. Furthermore, the Netfilter MIB has LastChanged objects for all Netfilter elements, which is a problem, because the original Netfilter subsystem does not have any timestamps. For this reason the data structures for Netfilter tables and chains had to be extended. This is a problem, because as mentioned before, these data structures are used by a userspace tool as well. So as a result, adding timestamps to tables and chains breaks compatibility and *iptables* produces strange errors when using it in combination with the new system. The solution is easy. Either we recompile the userspace tool with our new, altered kernel headers or we leave out the LastChanged objects. Finally, both ways were implemented and the system administrator can decide at kernel compile-time whether to include LastChange support and break backward compatibility or omit timestamps.

The Linux Netfilter subsystem was designed to be expandable so that kernel modules can add new tables. Comparable with the AgentX sublayer developed here, new modules have to register with the Netfilter module. The clean design and the split into several generic modules thereby helps that our network management extension automatically supports any new table extension.

```
static inline int
add_counter_to_entry(struct ipt_entry *e,
        const struct ipt_counters addme[],
        unsigned int *i)
{
        ADD_COUNTER(e->counters, addme[*i].bcnt, addme[*i].pcnt);
#ifdef CONFIG_AXNETFILTER_LC
        e->lastchange = jiffies;
#endif

        (*i)++;
        return 0;
}
```

Figure 4.3: Netfilter MIB: Example of a kernel subsystem function with management
        extension

Figure 4.3 shows a Netfilter function from ip_tables.c. This function already existed in the original Netfilter code but was extended with network management code. It increases the packet and byte counter of a rule and is called whenever an IP packet is matched by a rule. Because we would like to record the time of change the variable *lastchange* is updated whenever the counters are updated. As mentioned before, the addition of the variable *lastchange* to the Netfilter rule's data structure renders it incompatible with the userspace tool *iptables*. So this addition is optional and can be enabled or disabled at kernel compile-time.

Figure 4.4 shows an example of one of Netfilter's callback functions. It is responsible for the chain packet counters. This function is longer than its counterpart example from the IF-MIB because the Netfilter MIB uses more dynamic OIDs which get built on demand. Additional locking for the table and chain data structures also extend this function. The Netfilter MIB states the chain packet counter as read-only and so this function returns an error if *method* indicates a Set transaction. Depending on the kind of the request the function lnf_getnext_chain() tries to find the correct table and chain for a given OID or it looks for the next lexicographical successor. If a table and a chain could be located, the result OID is assembled. This OID, its variable type and the value of the chain's packet counter are reported back to the AgentX module.

The network management extension adds about 1,500 lines of code to the Netfilter subsystem, which is less than ten percent. Again, the main part is used for the implementation of the callback functions.

The current implementation lacks support for IPv6, which is mainly a copy & paste job and should be fairly easy to do. Write access is implemented for several objects, e.g., lnfRuleProtocol or lnfRuleSourceAddress. Additionally, you can delete any chain rule or append a rule via the RowStatus object lnfRuleStatus. RowStatus is a textual convention and is used to manage the creation and deletion of

```
int lnf_chainv4_pcounter(ax_oid *oid,
        ax_method method,
        char* context,
        ax_variable *res)
{
        struct ipt_table *table = NULL;
        struct ipt_entry *chain = NULL;

        if (!(method & GET))
                return AX_NOTWRITABLE;

        if (down_interruptible(&ipt_mutex) != 0) {
                printk("MUTEX problem\n");
                return AX_ERROR;
        }

        lnf_getnext_chain(oid, method, &table, &chain);

        if (((!chain) || (!getchainname(table, chain))) {
                up(&ipt_mutex);
                return AX_NOSUCHINSTANCE;
        }

        res->oid  = ax_oid_addint(V4CHAINT, 2); /*lnfChainPackets*/
        res->oid  = ax_oid_addint(res->oid, 1); /* ipv4(1) */
        res->oid  = ax_oid_addstring(res->oid,
                        table->name);
        res->oid  = ax_oid_addstring(res->oid,
                        getchainname(table, chain));
        res->value.counter64 = chain->counters.pcnt;
        res->type = AX_VB_COUNTER64;

        up(&ipt_mutex);
        return AX_SUCCESS;
}
```

Figure 4.4: Netfilter MIB: Callback function for `lnfChainPackets`

table rows. Additional information on this topic can be found in [16]. To append a rule, the new rule must set the RowStatus to `'createAndGo'` and the value of `lnfRuleIndex` must be higher than the highest index number in the current rule table.

## 4.3 Conclusions

For MIB implementors the procurement of data is facilitated since they have direct access to all data structures from within the kernel. However if we compare the kernel IF-MIB implementation to the userspace implementation of the NET-SNMP package one can say that the existing kernel interfaces to userspace provide the same information as the data structures in the kernel. So there is no immediate information gain by using kernel AgentX. Furthermore, MIB variables which are not exported into userspace are often not present in the kernel either. But because the subagent works inside the kernel, it may add those missing variables.

Notifications are an important way to notify the SNMP manger about system changes. Notification objects are rarely implemented in userspace agents because, aside from polling, the Linux kernel lacks methods to provide such information. With the Linux AgentX, framework Notifications can be implemented easily. This can be done either through existing kernel-internal notification functions or by adding small pieces of code to the functions that activate the change. Hence, Linux AgentX introduces a practical method for notifications for kernel subsystems.

Implementing network management inside the Linux kernel is a delicate task because one has the chance to mess up the whole operating system. Errors in userspace implementations do not affect system stability in the same way. Although a broken network management system could do enough damage as well, kernel subagents should be tested more thoroughly. Longer development cycles could be expected from kernel subagents implementations before they reach mature status.

AgentX kernel subagents can be implemented inside their kernel subsystems (Netfilter) or they can be attached to their subsystems as separate kernel modules (IF-MIB). The first method should be preferred because it has one big advantage. If the kernel subsystem and its network management code can be closely integrated, the development is put in the hand of the subsystem maintainer. He knows what features his subsystem can offer and how to take advantage of them in regard to network management. At the same time the AgentX module releases him from the necessity to know SNMP in detail. In the hand of one person, it is also unlikely that the kernel subsystem and its network management functions diverge.

# 5 Summary and outlook

*If you think you are too small to make a difference,*
*try sleeping in a closed room with a mosquito.*
— African proverb

Current SNMP agents retrieve kernel data via various interfaces and different formats from the operating system. These methods lack certain needs of a network management system. Especially a kernel-triggered notification mechanism and a simple transportation method for variable/value structures are missing. The AgentX implementation for the Linux kernel developed here supports both missing features and is suitable for the management of kernel internal components.

The Linux AgentX software is divided into two parts. On one hand, a generic AgentX sublayer which handles all major AgentX protocol tasks. And on the other hand, one or more kernel subagents with access to management information. The subagents connect through the AgentX sublayer to a master agent in userspace.

The implementation of a Management Information Base (MIB) inside the kernel does not necessarily result in a gain of information. Existing kernel interface often offer the same information as the kernel data structures. However, inside the kernel access to information is easier.

MIB implementations in userspace often neglect notification objects because they have no method to accurately detect status changes. Kernel subagents can use existing kernel-internal hooks or their own functions to detect these changes. This can be used to send notification messages.

Furthermore, AgentX kernel subagents can be implemented inside their kernel subsystems. That leads to the fact that the subsystem maintainer is responsible the system as a whole. Subsystem and network management features can be linked closely together.

With approximately 3,000 lines of code the Linux kernel AgentX implementation is not lightweight but reasonably small. Moreover it provides a cleanly designed interface to userspace and is easy to extend.

It is planned to release the Linux kernel AgentX software and get feedback from the network management and the Linux community.

Additionally, a complete implementation of one or more standard MIBs should be done, because the two MIBs implemented here are only partially complete or experimental. Finally, GetNext processing is by far the most difficult job for a MIB implementor. Unfortunately, it cannot be done in the AgentX module because it needs semantic knowledge of the MIB OIDs. But it may be worth to examine if it is possible to add new functions which can support MIB programmers with this problem.

Altogether the Linux AgentX network management framework represents a promising approach to improve SNMP support for kernel subsystems.

# A Abbreviations

| | |
|---|---|
| AgentX | AgentX Extensibility |
| ASN.1 | Abstract Syntax Notation One |
| BER | Basic Encoding Rules |
| CMIP | Common Management Information Protocol |
| CPU | Central Processing Unit |
| DPI | Distributed Program Interface |
| EMANATE | Enhanced Management Agent Through Extensions |
| HTTP | Hypertext Transfer Protocol |
| ICMP | Internet Control Message Protocol |
| IETF | Internet Engineering Task Force |
| IF-MIB | Interfaces MIB |
| IP | Internet Protocol (Version 4) |
| IPv6 | Internet Protocol Version 6 |
| IPC | Inter-Process Communication |
| LAN | Local Area Network |
| MIB | Management Information Base |
| MTU | Maximum Transfer Unit |
| NDA | Non Disclosure Agreement |
| OID | Object Identifier |
| PDU | Protocol Data Unit |
| RFC | Request For Comment |
| SMUX | SNMP Multiplexing |
| SNMP | Simple Network Management Protocol |
| TCP | Transmission Control Protocol |
| Varbind | Variable Binding |

# B  Manual pages

The following pages contain the manual pages for the Linux kernel AgentX subagents. These functions represent the interface between the AgentX sublayer and the MIB modules.

*Appendix B. Manual pages*

## NAME
ax_register - register a MIB region

## SYNOPSIS
**#include <agentx.h>**

**void ax_register(ax_session** *\*session*, **ax_register_table** *\*reg*);

**int ax_cb(ax_oid** *\*oid*, **ax_method** *method*, **char\*** *context*, **ax_variable** *\*var*);

## DESCRIPTION
**ax_register**() registers a MIB region with the master agent. *session* must contain a valid session pointer. Registering a MIB region always succeeds and does not depend on an established AgentX session with the master agent. So the real AgentX Register PDU may be sent later or even resent if a session has to be reconnected.

```
typedef struct _ax_register_table {
        ax_oid      root;      /* Root OID to register under */
        u_int8_t    timeout;   /* Timeout value in seconds */
        u_int8_t    priority;  /* Priority of this registration */
        u_int8_t    range;     /* SubID range*/
        u_int32_t   upper;     /* Upper bound */
        ax_register_cb *cb;    /* Pointer to callback table */
} ax_register_table;
```

The *timeout* value in seconds for the registration can be set in the register table or it can be inherited from the corresponding AgentX session if the value for *timeout* is zero. *priority* defines the precedence of this registration, when the master agent arbitrates between overlapping registrations from one or more sub-agents. It must hold a value between 1 (highest) and 255 (lowest priority). Aside the registration of MIB trees, the AgentX protocol also offers the registration of conceptual MIB table rows with a single registration request. This provides a general shorthand mechanism for specifying a MIB region. Thereby *root* defines the starting point of the MIB region. The end of the MIB region is calculated by taking the *root* OID and counting *range* identifiers from the left. This identifier is replaced with the *upper* bound variable. The variable *range* also indicates the kind of registration. A value of zero means the registration of a MIB tree. In this case, the *upper* bound variable can hold any value because it is not used. Any other value than zero in the variable *range* indicates MIB region allocation. The variable *cb* must point to a valid *ax_register_cb* structure.

```
typedef struct {
        ax_oid  suffix; /* OID Suffix relative to the Root OID */
        ax_cb   cb;     /* Callback function for MIB sub-tree */
} ax_register_cb;
```

One or more callback functions can be specified in the *ax_register_cb* table. Every *suffix* is appended to the *root* registration from the *ax_register_table* to determine the MIB tree for which the callback function *cb* is responsible. (see **EXAMPLE** section below). Requests to OIDs within the registered MIB tree but without a callback function are rejected with AX_NOSUCHOBJECT. The last entry in this table must contain NULL as callback function to denote the end of the table.

## RETURNCODES
Callback functions must return one of the following return codes.

**AX_SUCCESS**
> The request was completed successfully.

**AX_NOSUCHOBJECT**
> The requested variable does not match the object identifier prefix of any variable instantiated within the indicated context and session.

**AX_NOSUCHINSTANCE**
> The request variable does not exist and the condition for AX_NOSUCHOBJECT does not match.

**AX_RESOURCE**
> A resource could not be allocated.

**AX_NOTWRITABLE**
> A set request was refused because the given object is non-writable.

**AX_WRONGLENGTH**
> A set request was refused because it contained a value of wrong length for this variable.

**AX_WRONGTYPE**
> A set request was refused because it contained the wrong type for this variable.

**AX_WRONGVALUE**
> A set request was refused because it contained a value which can never be assigned to this variable.

**AX_NOCREATION**
> A set request was refused because it contained a variable which cannot be created.

**AX_INCONSISTENTNAME**
> A set request was refused because it contained a variable which does not exist and cannot be created under the present circumstances.

**AX_INCONSISTENTVALUE**
> A set request was refused because it contained a value which is presently inconsistent but could under other circumstances be held by the variable.

**AX_COMMITFAILED**
> A CommitSet request failed.

**AX_UNDOFAILED**
> An UndoSet request failed.

**AX_ERROR**
> The request failed because an error occurred which cannot be described otherwise.

ax_register(3x)                           Linux Kernel AgentX                           ax_register(3x)

**EXAMPLE**
    static ax_session *session = NULL;
    static ax_register_cb cbt[] = {
            {{ 3, {3, 2, 1}},   &cbfunc1 },
            {{ 2, {5, 5}},               &cbfunc2 },
            {{ 0, {}},                   NULL }
    };
    static ax_register_table regt = {
            root:               { 5, {1, 2, 3, 4, 5}},
            cb:                         (ax_register_cb *)&cbt,
            timeout:        0,
            lower:          0,
            upper:          0
    };

    /* We register 1.2.3.4.5 and have callback functions for
     *   1.2.3.4.5.3.2.1   ->   cbfunc1()
     *   1.2.3.4.5.5.5     ->   cbfunc2()
     */

    session = ax_session_open("Example MIB", 100, NULL);
    if (session)
            ax_register(session, &regt);

**BUGS**
    There is no ax_unregister(3). The only way to unregister a MIB region is to close the session, reopen it and
    to re-register any other regions again.

**SEE ALSO**
    **ax_session_open(3x)**

**AUTHOR**
    (C) 2002 Oliver Wellnitz <wellnitz@ibr.cs.tu-bs.de>, TU Braunschweig, Germany

## NAME

ax_session_open - create an AgentX session

## SYNOPSIS

#include <agentx.h>

ax_session *ax_session_open(char *descr, const u_int8_t timeout, ax_notify_cb notify);

void *ax_notify_cb(int notification, int error, void *data);

## DESCRIPTION

ax_session_open() creates a session with the master agent. It is described by string *descr* which is used in the AgentX Open PDU. *timeout* is the length of time, in seconds, that a master agent should allow to elapse after dispatching a message on a session before it regards the subagent as not responding.

The argument *notify* points to a function **ax_notify_cb** which gets notifications if the session status changes. It may be NULL if no notifications are needed.

**ax_notify_cb**() is a notification function implemented in the subagent. The argument *notify* shows the event that happened (see section **NOTIFICATIONS** below). Depending on the event, *error* may hold an optional error code and *data* may hold additional data.

## RETURN VALUE

ax_session_open() returns a pointer to a session handle on success, or NULL if an internal error occurred. This session handle is to be used in all further communications with the master agent.

## NOTIFICATIONS

The following list shows all events for which the **ax_notify_cb** function is called. Unless stated otherwise the arguments *error* and *data* do not have any meaning.

### AXN_SESSIONOPEN

The session was opened successfully.

### AXN_SESSIONFAILED

The session was refused by the master agent. *error* indicates the AgentX error sent by the master agent. *data* is a pointer to the corresponding **ax_register_table** structure.

### AXN_SESIONCLOSED

The session was closed by master agent or via /proc.

### AXN_REGISTERDONE

A requested **ax_register**() was successfully completed.

### AXN_REGISTERFAILED

A requested **ax_register**() finally failed. *error* indicates the AgentX error sent by the master agent.

## EXAMPLE

static ax_session *session = NULL;

session = ax_session_open("Example MIB", 100, NULL);

## SEE ALSO

**ax_session_close(3x)** , **ax_register(3x)**

**AUTHOR**
    (C) 2002 Oliver Wellnitz <wellnitz@ibr.cs.tu-bs.de>, IBR, TU Braunschweig, Germany

**NAME**

      ax_session_close - close an AgentX session

**SYNOPSIS**

      **#include <agentx.h>**

      **void ax_session_close(ax_session** *\*session*, **int** *reason*);

**DESCRIPTION**

      **ax_session_close**() closes a session, identified by session handle *session,* with the master agent.

**REASONS**

      There is currently only one value for *reason.*

      **AGENTX_CLOSE_SHUTDOWN**

            Sending entity is shutting down.

**EXAMPLE**

      static ax_session *session = NULL;

      session = ax_session_open("Example MIB", 100, NULL);
      ax_session_close(session, AGENTX_CLOSE_SHUTDOWN);

**SEE ALSO**

      **ax_session_open(3x)** , **ax_register(3x)**

**AUTHOR**

      (C) 2002 Oliver Wellnitz <wellnitz@ibr.cs.tu-bs.de>, TU Braunschweig, Germany

ax_time_now(3x)                     Linux Kernel AgentX                     ax_time_now(3x)

**NAME**
 ax_time_now - get the value of sysUptime.0
**SYNOPSIS**
 **#include <agentx.h>**

 **u_int32_t ax_time_now(void);**
**DESCRIPTION**
 This function returns the current value of sysUptime.0 as reported by the master agent. It utilizes a function
 to precisely predict this value in order to minimize communication with the master agent.

**SEE ALSO**
 **ax_time_jiffies(3x)**

**AUTHOR**
 (C) 2002 Oliver Wellnitz <wellnitz@ibr.cs.tu-bs.de>, TU Braunschweig, Germany

**NAME**
>  ax_time_jiffies - Transform jiffies into TimeTicks.

**SYNOPSIS**
>  #include <agentx.h>
>
>  u_int32_t ax_time_jiffies(unsigned long *j*);

**DESCRIPTION**
>  This function returns the value of sysUptime.0 at time *j*. If *j* is a time before the initialization of the master agent, zero is returned. If an overflow occurs, this function returns the maximum value for TimeTicks ($2^{32}-1$).

**SEE ALSO**
>  ax_time_now(3x)

**AUTHOR**
>  (C) 2002 Oliver Wellnitz <wellnitz@ibr.cs.tu-bs.de>, TU Braunschweig, Germany

ax_notify(3x)                   Linux Kernel AgentX                  ax_notify(3x)

## NAME

      ax_notify - Send AgentX Notify PDU

## SYNOPSIS

      **#include <agentx.h>**

      **ax_pdu \*ax_createpdu_notify(ax_session** *\*session***);**
      **int ax_send_pdu(ax_pdu** *\*pdu***);**
      **void ax_destroy_pdu(ax_pdu** *\*pdu***);**

## DESCRIPTION

      An AgentX Notify-PDU can be sent with these functions. The function **ax_createpdu_notify**() creates an
      PDU container for an Notify-PDU and fills in all necessary header information. Varbinds can be added with
      **ax_addvar_\***() functions. The function **ax_send_pdu**() actually sends the PDU and returns zero if it was
      successful and any value smaller than zero if not. Every PDU that was created with **ax_createpdu_notify**()
      has to be released with **ax_destroy_pdu().**

## SEE ALSO

      **ax_addvar(3x)**

## AUTHOR

      (C) 2002 Oliver Wellnitz <wellnitz@ibr.cs.tu-bs.de>, TU Braunschweig, Germany

ax_notify(3x)                       Linux Kernel AgentX                       ax_notify(3x)

## NAME
ax_addvar - Add varbind payload to an AgentX PDU

## SYNOPSIS
**#include <agentx.h>**

**void ax_addvar_vbcounter32(ax_pdu** *\*pdu*, **ax_oid** *oid*, **u_int32_t** *i*);
**void ax_addvar_vbcounter64(ax_pdu** *\*pdu*, **ax_oid** *oid*, **u_int64_t** *c64*);
**void ax_addvar_vbgauge32(ax_pdu** *\*pdu*, **ax_oid** *oid*, **u_int32_t** *i*);
**void ax_addvar_vbint(ax_pdu** *\*pdu*, **ax_oid** *oid*, **u_int32_t** *i*);
**void ax_addvar_vboid(ax_pdu** *\*pdu*, **ax_oid** *oid*, **ax_oid** *data*);
**void ax_addvar_vbstring(ax_pdu** *\*pdu*, **ax_oid** *oid*, **char** *\*data*);
**void ax_addvar_vbtt(ax_pdu** *\*pdu*, **ax_oid** *oid*, **u_int32_t** *i*);

## DESCRIPTION
These functions add variable bindings (varbinds) to a previously created AgentX PDU. Usually these functions are used to put values into a notification message. *pdu* is the AgentX packet where to add varbinds, *oid* is the name of the variable and the last argument is the value of the variable. The data is copied into the PDU, so that after calling **ax_addvar_vbstring** you may free it.

## TYPES
Use the following functions for these AgentX types:

**Integer**
         ax_addvar_vbint

**Octet String**
         ax_addvar_vbstring

**Object Identifier**
         ax_addvar_vboid

**IpAddress**
         ax_addvar_vbstring

**Counter32**
         ax_addvar_vbcounter32

**Gauge32**
         ax_addvar_vbgauge32

**TimeTicks**
         ax_addvar_vbtt

**Opaque**
         ax_addvar_vbstring

ax_notify(3x)                              Linux Kernel AgentX                              ax_notify(3x)

      **Counter64**
           ax_addvar_vbcounter64

**SEE ALSO**
      **ax_notify(3x)**

**AUTHOR**
      (C) 2002 Oliver Wellnitz <wellnitz@ibr.cs.tu-bs.de>, TU Braunschweig, Germany

## NAME

ax_oid - Create, manipulate and analyse object identifiers (OIDs)

## SYNOPSIS

#include <agentx.h>

ax_oid ax_oid_addoid(ax_oid *oid*, ax_oid *add*);
ax_oid ax_oid_addint(ax_oid *oid*, u_int32_t *i*);
ax_oid ax_oid_addstring(ax_oid *oid*, char *\*c*);
void ax_oid_copy(ax_oid *\*dest*, ax_oid *\*src*);
int ax_oid_length(ax_oid *\*oid*);
int ax_oid_data(ax_oid *\*oid*, int *pos*);
ax_oid ax_oid_del(ax_oid *oid*, int *n*);
int ax_oid_cmp(ax_oid *\*oid1*, ax_oid *\*oid2*);
int ax_oid_isprefix(ax_oid *\*prefix*, ax_oid *\*oid*);
char *ax_oid_makestring(ax_oid *oid*, int *pos*);
ax_oid ax_oid_addstring(ax_oid *oid*, char *\*c*);
int ax_oid_strcmp(char *\*a*, char *\*b*);

## DESCRIPTION

**ax_oid_addoid** adds an object identifier (OID) to another OID. If addition of both OIDs results in an over-long OID, no action is taken and the value of *oid* is returned.

**ax_oid_addint** adds an integer to an OID, thus increase its length by one digit. If the resulting OID is too long, no action is taken and *oid* is returned.

**ax_oid_addstring** adds an string to an OID. If the resulting OID is too long, no action is taken and *oid* is returned.

**ax_oid_copy** copies OID *src* to *dest*.

**ax_oid_del** reduces an OID by *n* digits. The last *digits* are cut off. If *n* is larger than the length of *oid* , no action is taken.

**ax_oid_length** returns the length of *oid* in digits.

**ax_oid_makestring;** decodes an octet string at position *pos*. If no valid octet string can be found, NULL is returned.

**ax_oid_data** returns the *n* th digit of *oid*. If *n* is larger than *oid*. -1 is returned. The first digit is addressed with *n* = 1.

**ax_oid_cmp** compares two oids. It returns an integer less than, equal to, or greater than zero if *oid1* is found, respectively, to be less than, to match or be greater than *oid2*.

**ax_oid_isprefix** returns 1 if *prefix* is an prefix of *oid* or 0 if not. If *prefix* is equal to *oid* 1 is returned.

**ax_oid_strcmp** compares two strings in OID-encoding. An OID-encoded string has its length at first place then followed by the string itself. This function returns an integer less than, equal to, or greater than zero if *a* is found, respectively, to be less than, to match or be greater than *b*.

**AUTHOR**
    (C) 2002 Oliver Wellnitz <wellnitz@ibr.cs.tu-bs.de>, TU Braunschweig, Germany

# C  TUBS IBR Linux Netfilter MIB

```
TUBS-IBR-LINUX-NETFILTER-MIB DEFINITIONS ::= BEGIN

-- @(#) $Id: nf-mib.tex,v 1.8 2002/09/05 02:29:43 wellnitz Exp $

IMPORTS
    MODULE-IDENTITY, OBJECT-TYPE, NOTIFICATION-TYPE,
    Unsigned32, Counter64
        FROM SNMPv2-SMI
    TEXTUAL-CONVENTION, TruthValue, StorageType, RowStatus, TimeStamp
        FROM SNMPv2-TC
    MODULE-COMPLIANCE, OBJECT-GROUP, NOTIFICATION-GROUP
        FROM SNMPv2-CONF
    SnmpAdminString
        FROM SNMP-FRAMEWORK-MIB
    InetAddressType, InetAddress, InetAddressPrefixLength
        FROM INET-ADDRESS-MIB
    ibr
        FROM TUBS-SMI;

lnfMIB MODULE-IDENTITY
    LAST-UPDATED "200207230000Z"
    ORGANIZATION "TU Braunschweig"
    CONTACT-INFO
        "Frank Strauss, Oliver Wellnitz
         TU Braunschweig
         Muehlenpfordtstrasse 23
         38106 Braunschweig
         Germany

         Tel: +49 531 391 3283
         Fax: +49 531 391 5936
         E-mail: {strauss,wellnitz}@ibr.cs.tu-bs.de"
    DESCRIPTION
        "Experimental MIB module for the Linux 2.4 netfilter
         subsystem."
    REVISION    "200207260000Z"
    DESCRIPTION
```

```
        "The initial revision of this module. This revision does
        not cover any match extensions and target extensions."
    ::= { ibr 13 }

--
-- The various groups defined within this MIB module:
--

lnfObjects      OBJECT IDENTIFIER ::= { lnfMIB 1 }

lnfTraps        OBJECT IDENTIFIER ::= { lnfMIB 2 }

lnfConformance OBJECT IDENTIFIER ::= { lnfMIB 3 }


--
-- Textual Conventions:
--

LnfTarget ::= TEXTUAL-CONVENTION
    STATUS          current
    DESCRIPTION
        "This data type represents an action that is about to
        be applied to a packet.

        none(1):   No action, except increasing counters.

        other(2):  An unknown extension action which cannot
                   be described by the values specified below.

        drop(3):   Drop the packet on the floor.

        accept(4): Let the packet through.

        queue(5):  Pass the packet to userspace.

        return(6): Stop traversing this chain and resume at the
                   next rule in the previous (calling) chain.

        chain(7):  Jump to the user chain specified by a
                   related object.
        "
    SYNTAX          INTEGER {
                        none(1),
                        other(2),
                        drop(3),
```

```
                    accept(4),
                    queue(5),
                    return(6),
                    chain(7)
                }

--
-- Object definitions:
--

lnfLastChange OBJECT-TYPE
    SYNTAX        TimeStamp
    MAX-ACCESS    read-only
    STATUS        current
    DESCRIPTION
        "The time of the last netfilter configuration change of any kind,
including any creation, deletion or modification of any table of this
MIB."
    ::= { lnfObjects 1 }

lnfTableTable OBJECT-TYPE
    SYNTAX        SEQUENCE OF LnfTableEntry
    MAX-ACCESS    not-accessible
    STATUS        current
    DESCRIPTION
        "A list of all tables installed on the netfilter subsystem."
    ::= { lnfObjects 2 }

lnfTableEntry OBJECT-TYPE
    SYNTAX        LnfTableEntry
    MAX-ACCESS    not-accessible
    STATUS        current
    DESCRIPTION
        "An entry describing a particular netfilter table."
    INDEX   { lnfTableAddressType, lnfTableName }
    ::= { lnfTableTable 1 }

LnfTableEntry ::=
    SEQUENCE {
        lnfTableAddressType            InetAddressType,
        lnfTableName                   SnmpAdminString,
        lnfTableLastChange             TimeStamp
    }

lnfTableAddressType OBJECT-TYPE
```

```
    SYNTAX      InetAddressType { ipv4(1), ipv6(2) }
    MAX-ACCESS  not-accessible
    STATUS      current
    DESCRIPTION
        "The address type for which the netfilter table works."
    ::= { lnfTableEntry 1 }

lnfTableName OBJECT-TYPE
    SYNTAX      SnmpAdminString (SIZE (0..32))
    MAX-ACCESS  not-accessible
    STATUS      current
    DESCRIPTION
        "The name of the netfilter table."
    ::= { lnfTableEntry 2 }

lnfTableLastChange OBJECT-TYPE
    SYNTAX      TimeStamp
    MAX-ACCESS  read-only
    STATUS      current
    DESCRIPTION
        "The time of the last modification of this netfilter
table, including the creation or deletion of a netfilter
chain that belongs to this table."
    ::= { lnfTableEntry 3 }

--


lnfChainTable OBJECT-TYPE
    SYNTAX      SEQUENCE OF LnfChainEntry
    MAX-ACCESS  not-accessible
    STATUS      current
    DESCRIPTION
        "A list of all chains installed on the netfilter
        subsystem."
    ::= { lnfObjects 3 }

lnfChainEntry OBJECT-TYPE
    SYNTAX      LnfChainEntry
    MAX-ACCESS  not-accessible
    STATUS      current
    DESCRIPTION
        "An entry describing a particular netfilter chain."
    INDEX   { lnfTableAddressType, lnfTableName, lnfChainName }
    ::= { lnfChainTable 1 }
```

```
LnfChainEntry ::=
    SEQUENCE {
        lnfChainName                          SnmpAdminString,
        lnfChainPackets                       Counter64,
        lnfChainOctets                        Counter64,
        lnfChainTarget                        LnfTarget,
        lnfChainLastChange                    TimeStamp,
        lnfChainStorage                       StorageType,
        lnfChainStatus                        RowStatus
    }

lnfChainName OBJECT-TYPE
    SYNTAX        SnmpAdminString (SIZE (0..32))
    MAX-ACCESS    not-accessible
    STATUS        current
    DESCRIPTION
        "The netfilter chain to which the rule belongs."
    ::= { lnfChainEntry 1 }

lnfChainPackets OBJECT-TYPE
    SYNTAX        Counter64
    MAX-ACCESS    read-only
    STATUS        current
    DESCRIPTION
        "The number of packets that passed this chain since
        the rule was installed or reset."
    ::= { lnfChainEntry 2 }

lnfChainOctets OBJECT-TYPE
    SYNTAX        Counter64
    MAX-ACCESS    read-only
    STATUS        current
    DESCRIPTION
        "The number of octets that passed this chain since
        the chain was installed or reset."
    ::= { lnfChainEntry 3 }

lnfChainTarget OBJECT-TYPE
    SYNTAX        LnfTarget { drop(3), accept(4), return(6) }
    MAX-ACCESS    read-create
    STATUS        current
    DESCRIPTION
        "The action that shall be applied to a packet if no rule
        within the chain matches. Note that user-defined chains
        only allow return(6)."
```

```
    DEFVAL      { return }
    ::= { lnfChainEntry 4 }

lnfChainLastChange OBJECT-TYPE
    SYNTAX      TimeStamp
    MAX-ACCESS  read-only
    STATUS      current
    DESCRIPTION
        "The time of the last modification of this netfilter
chain, including the creation or deletion of a netfilter
rule that belongs to this chain."
    ::= { lnfChainEntry 5 }

lnfChainStorage OBJECT-TYPE
    SYNTAX      StorageType
    MAX-ACCESS  read-create
    STATUS      current
    DESCRIPTION
        "This object defines whether this row is kept in
        volatile storage and lost upon reboot or whether it
        is backed up by stable storage or builtin."
    ::= { lnfChainEntry 6 }

lnfChainStatus OBJECT-TYPE
    SYNTAX      RowStatus
    MAX-ACCESS  read-create
    STATUS      current
    DESCRIPTION
        "This object is used to create and delete rows in the
        lnfChainTable."
    ::= { lnfChainEntry 7 }

--


lnfRuleTable OBJECT-TYPE
    SYNTAX      SEQUENCE OF LnfRuleEntry
    MAX-ACCESS  not-accessible
    STATUS      current
    DESCRIPTION
        "A list of all rules installed on the netfilter
        subsystem."
    ::= { lnfObjects 4 }

lnfRuleEntry OBJECT-TYPE
    SYNTAX      LnfRuleEntry
```

```
    MAX-ACCESS  not-accessible
    STATUS      current
    DESCRIPTION
        "An entry describing a particular netfilter rule. Rules
         of different netfilter tables and chains are
         distinguished by the corresponding index objects."
    INDEX   { lnfTableAddressType, lnfTableName,
              lnfChainName, lnfRuleIndex }
    ::= { lnfRuleTable 1 }

LnfRuleEntry ::=
    SEQUENCE {
        lnfRuleIndex                          Unsigned32,
        lnfRuleProtocol                       Unsigned32,
        lnfRuleProtocolInv                    TruthValue,
        lnfRuleSourceAddress                  InetAddress,
        lnfRuleSourceAddressPrefixLength      InetAddressPrefixLength,
        lnfRuleSourceAddressInv               TruthValue,
        lnfRuleDestinationAddress             InetAddress,
        lnfRuleDestinationAddressPrefixLength InetAddressPrefixLength,
        lnfRuleDestinationAddressInv          TruthValue,
        lnfRuleInInterface                    SnmpAdminString,
        lnfRuleInInterfaceInv                 TruthValue,
        lnfRuleOutInterface                   SnmpAdminString,
        lnfRuleOutInterfaceInv                TruthValue,
        lnfRuleFragment                       TruthValue,
        lnfRuleFragmentInv                    TruthValue,
        lnfRulePackets                        Counter64,
        lnfRuleOctets                         Counter64,
        lnfRuleTarget                         LnfTarget,
        lnfRuleTargetChain                    SnmpAdminString,
        lnfRuleTrapEnable                     TruthValue,
        lnfRuleLastChange                     TimeStamp,
        lnfRuleStorage                        StorageType,
        lnfRuleStatus                         RowStatus
    }

lnfRuleIndex OBJECT-TYPE
    SYNTAX      Unsigned32
    MAX-ACCESS  not-accessible
    STATUS      current
    DESCRIPTION
        "A unique number identifying the rule within a netfilter
         chain."
    ::= { lnfRuleEntry 1 }
```

65

```
lnfRuleProtocol OBJECT-TYPE
    SYNTAX      Unsigned32 (0..255)
    MAX-ACCESS  read-create
    STATUS      current
    DESCRIPTION
        "The protocol of the rule. The number zero matches all
         protocols."
    DEFVAL      { 0 }
    ::= { lnfRuleEntry 2 }

lnfRuleProtocolInv OBJECT-TYPE
    SYNTAX      TruthValue
    MAX-ACCESS  read-create
    STATUS      current
    DESCRIPTION
        "This flag specifies whether the lnfRuleProtocol test
         has to be inverted."
    DEFVAL      { false }
    ::= { lnfRuleEntry 3 }

lnfRuleSourceAddress OBJECT-TYPE
    SYNTAX      InetAddress
    MAX-ACCESS  read-create
    STATUS      current
    DESCRIPTION
        "The source address of a packet. The exact format depends
         on the address type specified by lnfRuleAddressType.
         This test is applied for an address prefix whose length
         is specified by lnfRuleSourceAddressPrefixLength.

         If a new row is created this object should default to
         an all-zeros value with a length approrpiate for the
         corresponding lnfRuleAddressType object value."
    ::= { lnfRuleEntry 4 }

lnfRuleSourceAddressPrefixLength OBJECT-TYPE
    SYNTAX      InetAddressPrefixLength
    MAX-ACCESS  read-create
    STATUS      current
    DESCRIPTION
        "The network prefix length associated with
         lnfRuleSourceAddress."
    DEFVAL      { 0 }
    ::= { lnfRuleEntry 5 }
```

```
lnfRuleSourceAddressInv OBJECT-TYPE
    SYNTAX       TruthValue
    MAX-ACCESS   read-create
    STATUS       current
    DESCRIPTION
        "This flag specifies whether the lnfRuleSourceAddress
        and lnfRuleSourceAddressPrefixLength test has to
        be inverted."
    DEFVAL       { false }
    ::= { lnfRuleEntry 6 }

lnfRuleDestinationAddress OBJECT-TYPE
    SYNTAX       InetAddress
    MAX-ACCESS   read-create
    STATUS       current
    DESCRIPTION
        "The destination address of a packet. The exact format
        depends on the address type specified by
        lnfRuleAddressType. This test is applied for an address
        prefix whose length is specified by
        lnfRuleDestinationAddressPrefixLength.

        If a new row is created this object should default to
        an all-zeros value with a length approrpiate for the
        corresponding lnfRuleAddressType object value."
    ::= { lnfRuleEntry 7 }

lnfRuleDestinationAddressPrefixLength OBJECT-TYPE
    SYNTAX       InetAddressPrefixLength
    MAX-ACCESS   read-create
    STATUS       current
    DESCRIPTION
        "The network prefix length associated with
        lnfRuleDestinationAddress."
    DEFVAL       { 0 }
    ::= { lnfRuleEntry 8 }

lnfRuleDestinationAddressInv OBJECT-TYPE
    SYNTAX       TruthValue
    MAX-ACCESS   read-create
    STATUS       current
    DESCRIPTION
        "This flag specifies whether the lnfRuleDestinationAddress
        and lnfRuleDestinationAddressPrefixLength test has to
```

```
            be inverted."
        DEFVAL      { false }
        ::= { lnfRuleEntry 9 }

lnfRuleInInterface OBJECT-TYPE
    SYNTAX      SnmpAdminString (SIZE (0..16))
    MAX-ACCESS  read-create
    STATUS      current
    DESCRIPTION
        "Name of an interface via which a packet is going to be
         received (only for packets entering the INPUT, FORWARD and
         PREROUTING chains).  If the interface name ends in a '+',
         then any interface which begins with this name will match.
         If this is an empty string, any interface name will match."
    DEFVAL      { "" }
    ::= { lnfRuleEntry 10 }

lnfRuleInInterfaceInv OBJECT-TYPE
    SYNTAX      TruthValue
    MAX-ACCESS  read-create
    STATUS      current
    DESCRIPTION
        "This flag specifies whether the lnfRuleInInterface test
         has to be inverted."
    DEFVAL      { false }
    ::= { lnfRuleEntry 11 }

lnfRuleOutInterface OBJECT-TYPE
    SYNTAX      SnmpAdminString (SIZE (0..16))
    MAX-ACCESS  read-create
    STATUS      current
    DESCRIPTION
        "Name of an interface via which a packet is going to be
         sent (for packets entering the FORWARD, OUTPUT and
         POSTROUTING chains).  If the interface name ends in a '+',
         then any interface which begins with this name will match.
         If this is an empty string, any interface name will match."
    DEFVAL      { "" }
    ::= { lnfRuleEntry 12 }

lnfRuleOutInterfaceInv OBJECT-TYPE
    SYNTAX      TruthValue
    MAX-ACCESS  read-create
    STATUS      current
    DESCRIPTION
```

```
            "This flag specifies whether the lnfRuleOutInterface test
             has to be inverted."
      DEFVAL      { false }
      ::= { lnfRuleEntry 13 }

lnfRuleFragment OBJECT-TYPE
      SYNTAX       TruthValue
      MAX-ACCESS   read-create
      STATUS       current
      DESCRIPTION
            "If this flag is true, the rule only refers to second and
             further fragments of fragmented packets.  Since there is
             no way to tell the source or destination ports of such a
             packet (or ICMP type), such a packet will not match any
             rules which specify them."
      DEFVAL      { false }
      ::= { lnfRuleEntry 14 }

lnfRuleFragmentInv OBJECT-TYPE
      SYNTAX       TruthValue
      MAX-ACCESS   read-create
      STATUS       current
      DESCRIPTION
            "This flag specifies whether the lnfRuleFragmentInv test,
             if true, has to be inverted. An inverted rule will only
             match head fragments, or unfragmented packets."
      DEFVAL      { false }
      ::= { lnfRuleEntry 15 }

lnfRulePackets OBJECT-TYPE
      SYNTAX       Counter64
      MAX-ACCESS   read-only
      STATUS       current
      DESCRIPTION
            "The number of packets that matched this rule since
             the rule was installed or reset."
      ::= { lnfRuleEntry 16 }

lnfRuleOctets OBJECT-TYPE
      SYNTAX       Counter64
      MAX-ACCESS   read-only
      STATUS       current
      DESCRIPTION
            "The number of octets that matched this rule since the
             rule was installed or reset."
```

```
    ::= { lnfRuleEntry 17 }

lnfRuleTarget OBJECT-TYPE
    SYNTAX        LnfTarget
    MAX-ACCESS    read-create
    STATUS        current
    DESCRIPTION
        "The action that shall be applied to a packet if the
        rule matches. If the value is chain(7), then jump to
        the user chain specified by lnfRuleTargetChain."
    DEFVAL        { none }
    ::= { lnfRuleEntry 18 }

lnfRuleTargetChain OBJECT-TYPE
    SYNTAX        SnmpAdminString (SIZE (0..32))
    MAX-ACCESS    read-create
    STATUS        current
    DESCRIPTION
        "The name of the target chain if the value of
        lnfRuleTarget is chain(7)."
    ::= { lnfRuleEntry 19 }

lnfRuleTrapEnable  OBJECT-TYPE
    SYNTAX        TruthValue
    MAX-ACCESS    read-write
    STATUS        current
    DESCRIPTION
        "Indicates whether lnfRuleMatch traps should be
        generated for packets matching this rule. Note
        that it's up to the implementation to delay and
        accumulate mutliple traps in order to reduce the
        number of emitted traps."
    DEFVAL        { false }
    ::= { lnfRuleEntry 20 }

lnfRuleLastChange OBJECT-TYPE
    SYNTAX        TimeStamp
    MAX-ACCESS    read-only
    STATUS        current
    DESCRIPTION
        "The time of the last modification of this netfilter rule.
If it has been unchanged since the last re-initialization
of the local network management subsystem, then this
        object contains a zero value."
    ::= { lnfRuleEntry 21 }
```

```
lnfRuleStorage OBJECT-TYPE
    SYNTAX      StorageType
    MAX-ACCESS  read-create
    STATUS      current
    DESCRIPTION
        "This object defines whether this row is kept in
        volatile storage and lost upon reboot or whether it
        is backed up by stable storage or builtin."
    ::= { lnfRuleEntry 22 }

lnfRuleStatus OBJECT-TYPE
    SYNTAX      RowStatus
    MAX-ACCESS  read-create
    STATUS      current
    DESCRIPTION
        "This object is used to create and delete rows in the
        lnfRuleTable."
    ::= { lnfRuleEntry 23 }

--
-- Notifications:
--

lnfNotifications OBJECT IDENTIFIER ::= { lnfTraps 0 }

lnfRuleMatch NOTIFICATION-TYPE
    OBJECTS     { lnfRulePackets, lnfRuleOctets }
    STATUS      current
    DESCRIPTION
        "A lnfRuleMatch trap signifies that the rule to which
        the lnfRulePackets and lnfRuleOctets objects belong
        was matched by at least one packets since the last
        trap for the same rule was emitted.

        The agent may delay and accumulate mutliple traps in order
        to reduce the number of emitted traps, but the time for
        accumulation should be no more than 60 seconds.

        Note that detailed information on the packet(s) that
        triggered a trap is not available from the trap's
        objects. This would cause problems with the accumulation
        of matches and/or increased trap traffic."
    ::= { lnfNotifications 1 }
```

```
--
-- Conformance statements:
--

lnfCompliances OBJECT IDENTIFIER ::= { lnfConformance 1 }

lnfGroups OBJECT IDENTIFIER ::= { lnfConformance 2 }

lnfCompliance MODULE-COMPLIANCE
    STATUS       current
    DESCRIPTION
        "The compliance statement for an SNMP entity which
         implements the Linux Netfilter MIB."
    MODULE       -- this module
    MANDATORY-GROUPS { lnfGeneralGroup, lnfNotificationGroup }

--     OBJECT       lnfTableAddressType
--         SYNTAX       InetAddressType { ipv4(1), ipv6(2) }
--         DESCRIPTION
--         "Other address types than IPv4 and IPv6 are not required."

    ::= { lnfCompliances 1 }

lnfGeneralGroup OBJECT-GROUP
    OBJECTS {
        lnfLastChange,

        lnfTableLastChange,

        lnfChainPackets, lnfChainOctets, lnfChainTarget,
        lnfChainLastChange, lnfChainStorage, lnfChainStatus,

        lnfRuleProtocol, lnfRuleProtocolInv,
        lnfRuleSourceAddress, lnfRuleSourceAddressPrefixLength,
        lnfRuleSourceAddressInv, lnfRuleDestinationAddress,
        lnfRuleDestinationAddressPrefixLength,
        lnfRuleDestinationAddressInv, lnfRuleInInterface,
        lnfRuleInInterfaceInv, lnfRuleOutInterface,
        lnfRuleOutInterfaceInv, lnfRuleFragment,
        lnfRuleFragmentInv, lnfRulePackets, lnfRuleOctets,
        lnfRuleTarget, lnfRuleTargetChain, lnfRuleTrapEnable,
        lnfRuleLastChange, lnfRuleStorage, lnfRuleStatus
    }
    STATUS       current
    DESCRIPTION
```

```
            "A collection of all Linux Netfilter objects of
            the core table."
        ::= { lnfGroups 1 }

lnfNotificationGroup NOTIFICATION-GROUP
        NOTIFICATIONS {
            lnfRuleMatch
        }
        STATUS       current
        DESCRIPTION
            "A collection of all Linux Netfilter notifications."
        ::= { lnfGroups 2 }

END
```

# Bibliography

[1] J. Case, R. Mundy, D. Partain, and B. Stewart. Introduction to Version 3 of the Internet-standard Network Management Framework. RFC 2570, SNMP Research, TIS Labs at Network Associates, Ericsson, Cisco Systems, April 1999.

[2] The NET-SNMP home page. WWW Page. http://www.net-snmp.org.

[3] B. Hebrawi. *OSI Upper Layer Standards and Practices*. McGraw–Hill, 1992.

[4] SNMP – Simple Network Managment Protocol. WWW Page. http://www.rad.com/networks/1995/snmp/snmp.htm.

[5] M. T. Rose. *The Simple Book – An Introduction to Internet Management, Revised Second Edition*. Prentice Hall, 2 edition, 1996.

[6] D. Perkins and E. McGinnis. *Understanding SNMP MIBs*. Prentice Hall, 1997.

[7] M. Daniele, B. Wijnen, M. Ellison, and D. Francisco. Agent Extensibility (AgentX) Protocol Version 1. RFC 2741, Digital Equipment Corporation, IBM T. J. Watson Research, Ellison Software Consulting, Cisco Systems, January 2000.

[8] J. Postel. Internet Control Message Protocol. RFC 792, ISI, September 1981.

[9] K. McCloghrie, D. Perkins, J. Schönwälder, J. Case, M. Rose, and S. Waldbusser. Conformance Statements for SMIv2. RFC 2580, Cisco Systems, SNMPinfo, TU Braunschweig, SNMP Research, First Virtual Holdings, SNMP Research, International Network Services, April 1999.

[10] M. Rose. SNMP MUX Protocol and MIB. RFC 1227, Performance Systems International, May 1991.

[11] G. Carpenter and B. Wijnen. SNMP-DPI: Simple Network Management Protocol Distributed Program Interface. RFC 1228, T.J. Watson Research Center, IBM Corp., May 1991.

[12] B. Wijnen, G. Carpenter, K. Curran, A. Sehgal, and G. Waters. Simple Network Management Protocol Distributed Protocol Interface Version 2.0. RFC 1592, IBM T.J. Watson Research Center, Bell Northern Research Ltd., March 1994.

[13] EMANATE product. WWW Page. http://www.snmp.com/products/emanate.html.

[14] Daniel P. Bovet and Marco Cesati. *Understanding the Linux Kernel*. O'Reilly, 2000.

[15] Alessandro Rubini and Jonathan Corbet. *Linux Device Drivers*. O'Reilly, 2nd edition, 2001.

[16] K. McCloghrie, D. Perkins, J. Schönwälder, J. Case, M. Rose, and S. Waldbusser. Textual Conventions for SMIv2. RFC 2579, Cisco Systems, SNMPinfo, TU Braunschweig, SNMP Research, First Virtual Holdings, International Network Services, April 1999.

[17] K. McCloghrie and F. Kastenholz. The Interfaces Group MIB. RFC 2863, Cisco Systems, Argon Networks, June 2000.

[18] Pat Eyler. *Networking Linux: A Practical Guide to TCP/IP*. New Riders Professional Library, 2001.

[19] iptables(1) - ip packet filter administration. manual page, August 2000.

# Wissenschaftlicher Buchverlag bietet

kostenfreie

# Publikation

von aktuellen

# wissenschaftlichen Arbeiten

Diplomarbeiten, Magisterarbeiten, Master und Bachelor Theses
sowie Dissertationen und wissenschaftliche Monographien

## innerhalb von Fachbuchprojekten (Monographien und Sammelwerke)

**in den Fachgebieten Wirtschafts- und Sozialwissenschaften
sowie Wirtschaftsinformatik.**

Sie verfügen über eine Arbeit zu aktuellen Fragestellungen aus den genannten
Fachgebieten, die hohen inhaltlichen und formalen Ansprüchen genügt,
und haben **Interesse an einer honorarvergüteten Publikation**?

Dann senden Sie bitte erste Informationen über sich und Ihre Arbeit per Email
an info@vdm-verlag.de. Unser Außenlektorat meldet sich umgehend bei Ihnen.

VDM Verlag Dr. Mueller e.K. · Dudweiler Landstraße 125a
D - 66123 Saarbrücken · www.vdm-buchverlag.de

www.ingramcontent.com/pod-product-compliance
Lightning Source LLC
LaVergne TN
LVHW080102070326
832902LV00014B/2385